House-tr
Your Dog

A KENNEL CLUB BOOK®

DEDICATION

This book is unashamedly dedicated to a dog. My dog. Her name is Ginger. She's a 17-year-old Toy Poodle. We've been together since she was 8 weeks old and I was 17 years younger.

She has been my constant companion, my hiking and biking buddy, my protector, my confidante, my cuddle partner. She has listened to my complaints and worries about life's difficult matters as well as my celebrations of its joys and thrills. She has always been trusted to receive my confessions of the heart. She has never judged me for anything I've done nor has she held a grudge for actions I've taken or things I've forgotten to do. She has been my life's perfect partner.

I know our days together are numbered now and I spend mine trying to make her life as comfortable as possible. She's blind and deaf now. I am her eyes and ears. I consider that a privilege, not a burden, for she has given her total being to my comfort and happiness these many years.

When the day comes that she leaves me, I will miss her. However, I know she'll become an angel and we'll meet again one day at the Rainbow Bridge. Thus I say, "Thanks for making my life so wonderful, Ginger. I will always love you."

Photographs by
Bernd Brinkmann, Isabelle Français,
Carol Ann Johnson, Alice van Kempen
and Michael Trafford

KENNEL CLUB BOOKS® HOUSE-TRAINING YOUR DOG
ISBN: 1-59378-424-4

Copyright © 2005, **2007** • Kennel Club Books® • A Division of BowTie, Inc.
40 Broad Street, Freehold, NJ 07728 USA
Cover Design Patented: US 6,435,559 B2 • Printed in South Korea

10 9 8 7 6 5 4 3 2

House-training Your Dog

By Charlotte Schwartz

Contents

House-training Your Dog

What an exciting time when you welcome a new puppy into your home! Take time to enjoy it, but be prepared for the work ahead.

INTRODUCTION

Congratulations! There's a new dog in your life, and that's exciting. Maybe he's a tiny puppy, a mere eight weeks old. Or perhaps he's an adult dog that needed a new home and you adopted him. Either way, the immediate future will be a period of adjustment for you, your family and your new house dog.

First, you'll need to learn what the dog's needs are, how they relate to you and your lifestyle and, most importantly, how you can make the necessary adjustments so this new member of the family becomes a success story, not a failure. The dog will need to learn about you and the other members of his family. And when he does, he'll have to adjust to your schedule and habits. All members of the family will have to be patient and cooperative as this whole process evolves into a cohesive domestic unit. Finally, the children must learn how to play gently with the dog so that he never learns how to be rough and aggressive.

Things such as meal schedules, grooming, play times, obedience training practice and, of course, house-training will

This Chihuahua may be small, but even small puddles in the house are a big problem! Toy dogs can be challenging to train but make very rewarding companions.

occupy the next several weeks until you and the dog become accustomed to each other. There will be lots of learning involved—some new lessons to learn, maybe some old habits to break. But with patience, love and understanding, you can create a magical, rewarding experience for all concerned.

Let's say the dog you've chosen is an adult. You liked him the moment you saw him and now he's yours. At first, he may miss his previous owners, but soon he'll learn to love you because the two of you are building a bond together. One of the first things you'll need to do is house-train him. He may or may not have been house-trained in his former home, but moving into your house is a new experience and he's not sure when or where to relieve himself.

This book is written to make that process quick and easy for you and your dog. By helping you understand what the dog thinks about relieving himself, you'll find that house-training isn't the big impossible monster that many people make it out to be. You'll also have your new friend understanding the difference between going outdoors to play and going outdoors to relieve himself. And you'll do it all faster than you ever thought possible— and learn a lot about your dog in the process.

Whether pup or adult, all dogs can and must be house-trained. The method varies slightly depending on the age of the dog, but consistency is the key.

LICK AND SPAN

At birth, dogs, whether wild or domesticated, cannot void by themselves, so their mother cleans them and consumes their droppings. This act keeps the den clean, and the puppies learn not to soil their sleeping areas right from birth. By four to five weeks of age, they begin to eliminate independently away from the nest or den. Take advantage of the dog's desire to eliminate away from his den by using this natural instinct to house-train the puppy quickly and easily.

We've been talking here about house-training adult dogs. Now let's address the subject of house-training puppies. That's another whole ball of fur!

Puppies usually arrive in their new homes anywhere between 8 and 20 weeks of age. They're warm, cuddly, friendly and cute, and they seem to leak constantly! As a matter of fact, a ten-week-old puppy will urinate about every hour, if not more frequently. The 16-week-old puppy can hold it longer, but, like his younger friend, he doesn't tell you when he has to go. He just squats whenever and wherever he chooses. No matter how hard you try to teach him to give you a signal when he needs to void, he doesn't have a clue about warning you of his impending needs. That

Your new puppy comes with lots of cuddles—along with the inevitable puddles!

In addition to creature comforts like a cozy bed and toys, the structure of the house rules and a daily schedule are what will make a puppy feel confident and secure in his new home.

just seems to be a behavior that's not on his agenda.

Unlike the adult dog, the puppy must develop a whole range of lifestyle habits that fit your family while making almost daily adjustments to his growing body. That's a big order for a little fellow. He'll need your patience and understanding now more than ever if he's to grow up to be a fine canine companion. Unlike the adult dog, the puppy will have no old habits that need correcting. Instead, he'll rely on you to show him how to fit into your lifestyle. At this early age, the puppy will learn each lesson with ease and eagerness.

Structure is key to the puppy's lifestyle. You must establish meal times, grooming times, play times, rest times, even the cuddle times that most puppies love. There are obedience lessons and good manners to learn, but most pressing of all are the house-training lessons.

This book was written for you and your new dog or puppy: it is a true bathroom reader! It contains chapters about training puppies as well as sections focusing on adult dogs and problem-solving. Whatever your need, this book offer a series of constructive, productive measures and methods to help you help your new friend become house-trained quickly and reliably.

ELIMINATION RULES

Controlling his elimination habits is the very first lesson that a puppy receives in life. The learning begins with his mother in the nest and continues when he takes up residence in your home. Consequently, it's extremely important that the people in the dog's new human pack remain as consistent in the rules of cleanliness as his mother was.

Dogs are den animals and they love the security of a crate. For those who doubt, just look at this Brittany, resting comfortably in his own special area and feeling right at home.

Understanding the Basics

DOG THOUGHTS

Whenever we try to teach a dog something, we need to figure out what the dog thinks about the matter. This isn't as easy as it may sound. Dogs can't tell us, for example, how they feel about learning when and where to relieve themselves. Consequently, we can only surmise what they think about this basic natural function, if they think anything about it at all.

If we could ever talk to a dog about it, we might in fact find out that dogs give practically no thought to urinating and defecating. It's a normal bodily function and they, like other mammals, have very little to do with the urge to "go." When it comes on, the body naturally relieves itself and normal activities resume.

Since humans bring dogs into their homes, however, dogs must learn what is and is not acceptable when it comes to the matter of relief. Most people want the dog to relieve himself outdoors. In some cases, with very small dogs, owners want their tidy tiny pets to use special areas of the home for this purpose. Incontinence

When it comes to toileting, it's just a bodily function for dogs. They know they have to do it but they don't put much, if any, thought into it!

It's a happy owner whose dog is acclimated to clean indoor living and reliable in his habits around the home.

pads, newspapers, cat-litter boxes are all items sometimes used by toy-dog owners for house-training.

In other circumstances, some people, perhaps women or the elderly, who live alone, especially in big cities, may be apprehensive about going outside to walk their dogs at night. Thus training the dog to paper is a practical solution for personal safety and peace of mind. Such cautious people may choose a bathroom or a laundry or utility room for the dog's relief area. As long as the dog understands what is acceptable and the owner keeps the door open at all times so the dog has access to his spot, indoor house-training works well.

Only small and/or toy dogs are suitable for this indoor routine. Teaching a large-breed puppy to relieve himself indoors would not be very practical when he's six months old. The amount of urine and feces that a large dog produces would be inconvenient when it comes to cleanup.

Your dog probably doesn't think much about voiding. However, a dog can be trained to recognize when he feels the urge to go and how to communicate that feeling to you, his owner. That's the secret to house-training:

If you have a yard, you will walk your dog there on leash to show him the relief site you've chosen. If no yard is available, you will always take your dog out for on-leash walks at potty times.

Plan a feeding and elimination schedule that is appropriate for your dog and also fits into the flow of your daily schedule and the household routine.

teaching the dog to communicate with you and not relieve himself in inappropriate places.

FEEDING TIMES

When you feed the dog influences when he needs to relieve himself. Regardless of whether you're house-training a puppy or an adult dog, the feeding schedule makes a difference. Generally speaking, food is passed between three and six hours after the dog eats. The amount of time between ingesting food and passing it varies widely for many reasons. The type of food ingested, the

amount ingested, the dog's own individual metabolism and the dog's activities during the period of digestion all play a part in the body's need to void.

For example, when the dog is physically active, the body runs on "fast forward" to keep pace. Body functions react much more rapidly than when the dog is quiet and at rest. When the body senses "idle time," bodily functions slow down. In that case, matter moves more slowly through the digestive system, prolonging the voiding process. Thus a brisk walk or a run-and-retrieve play session can bring on the dog's need to void, while a night's sleep slows things down so the dog doesn't feel the need to pass his food so quickly.

The same routine applies to water consumption, too. Therefore, it's prudent to restrict the intake of water in the later evening hours. If the dog consumes large amounts of water between dinner and bedtime, chances are you'll be getting up several times during the night because the dog wants "out." Always make water available to the dog, but limit the amount in the evening. A few sips now and then or offering him an ice cube to lick can satiate his thirst while it does not overload his kidneys and bladder.

Putting the dog on a scheduled feeding plan is, for many reasons, the best way to control the dog's elimination times. Young puppies usually require three meals a day, but that phase passes quickly. Before you know it, puppy will be old enough to switch to a twice-daily feeding schedule, one meal in the morning and one in the evening. Adult dogs should also be on a two-meal-a-day program.

Serving large quantities of food at one time, such as just one big daily meal, overloads the dog's digestive system and can cause diarrhea, stomach upset and great discomfort. What's even worse, gastric torsion (or bloat) can result

Physical activity stimulates a dog's need to void. It's not uncommon for a dog to relieve himself during a play session or right afterwards.

when the stomach flips over and prevents food and gases from escaping through the intestines or mouth. Large-breed dogs are more prone to bloat than small-breed dogs, though any dog can suffer gastric torsion. It is a life-threatening condition that must be surgically treated immediately.

The two-meal-a-day plan is the best for maintaining good health in the dog and is also the most convenient plan for owners. Most people are home in the early morning and again in the early evening, so feeding the dog at those times proves convenient for all. Once you establish a regular feeding schedule for your dog,

DIGESTION COURSE
It can take up to 18 hours for the dog's food to be fully digested. Thus, if the puppy swallows a non-food item, carefully examine each stool for several days afterward to be sure he passes the item.

Over the years, the author has lived with many dogs, both small and large ones, and it's apparent that they usually void first thing in the morning and again following their evening meals. All of them have been fed two meals a day since reaching five months of age. As for the very young ones, eating three or more meals a day, they void more often. Fortunately, this pattern of frequency is short-lived, and they move on to a more reasonable and predictable schedule very soon.

Just remember that when you give a dog food, he will need to pass it sometime in the near future. The smart owner sets a routine that's convenient for his own schedule so that he's there for meal times and also for potty breaks. Feeding times definitely influence relieving times.

All of the pups' needs are taken care of by the breeder before the pups are old enough to leave for new homes. whether puppy or adult, you can then begin to observe the times when the dog passes his stool. By being aware of your dog's elimination habits, you can plan the times when he needs to be taken out for walks.

Relieving themselves outdoors, away from their living quarters, is a natural instinct for dogs of all ages.

CANINE RELIEF HABITS

One of the main reasons that dogs have become man's best friend over the years is the fact that they are naturally clean animals. Domestic farm animals usually relieve themselves whenever and wherever they feel the urge. Dogs, on the other hand, are fussy about their relief areas. For example, dogs will not soil their sleeping or eating areas. By utilizing this basic instinct of cleanliness, we can teach the dog when and where to relieve himself in a manner that also suits the owner.

House-training the puppy is made simple due to the dog's need to keep his resting area clean. Crate-training is the obvious method used to produce quick and painless results for both owner and dog. In certain cases, such as with an adult dog who has never been crate-trained, using a crate may not be feasible. The dog may be just too big to fit comfortably into a crate that fits within your living space. Or he may be so upset at the confinement of a crate that he simply cannot tolerate it. No amount of coaxing or bribing with treats can change his mind, so you are forced to find an alternative solution to provide him with his own resting area. Likewise, certain large-breed puppies should not be crate-trained, as the confinement may hinder healthy bone and joint development. In such cases, confining the dog to a small but open area

The feeding schedule and relief schedule go hand in hand. Young pups have to "go" soon after eating or drinking, so you must plan accordingly.

and giving him soft bedding may prove to be the better option.

Whatever you decide to use as the dog's sleeping area, the size of it will be the key factor in achieving success. The area must be roomy enough for the dog to lie down, stretch out, sit up and stand up without his head hitting the top, yet small enough so that he cannot relieve himself at one end and sleep at the other end, far away from his excrement.

The dog will not lie down and sleep in his own droppings. Therefore, if you offer the dog frequent opportunities to relieve himself outside his quarters, the dog quickly learns that the outdoors (or the paper indoors) is the place to go when he needs to

MY OWN LITTLE CORNER

Your dog considers his crate as his private den. In the wild, dogs seek out small, warm, dark places in which to rest and feel secure. When his crate replicates a den, he happily uses it for similar purposes. You, on the other hand, should see the crate as a place of safety for you, for the dog and for your home. That's a win/win situation!

urinate or defecate. It also reinforces his innate instinct to keep his sleeping area clean. In addition, it helps to develop the muscle control that will eventually produce clean living habits. Finally, it provides safety for the dog and for your home.

Most dogs like wire crates because they can see all that's going on around them. With cozy padding, a small treat and a favorite toy, he will settle right into his "home within a home."

CRATES

Crates can be made of wire, nylon mesh or fiberglass, the latter often referred to as airline-type. The crate should be lined with a clean towel, never a stuffed cushion type of bed, as this will give the dog an opportunity to destroy the bedding and you'll have stuffing everywhere! If the dog chews up the towel, it can be easily replaced. Eventually the dog will grow out of the "chewing up his towel" phase and, as he matures and becomes accustomed to his crate or "cubby," you can replace the towel with a soft cushion or crate pad.

The three most common crate types: mesh (left), wire (right) and fiberglass.

Never line his sleeping area with newspaper. Puppy litters are usually raised on newspaper and, once in your home, the puppy will immediately associate newspaper with voiding. Never put newspaper on any floor while house-training the dog to go outdoors, as this will only confuse the dog. If you're paper-training the dog, use paper in the designated relief area only.

The crate should be placed in an area of your home where much of the family activity takes place—the kitchen, the family room, the room where family members gather most of the time. The kitchen is ideal, since the floor is cleanable; if your family room is not carpeted, then that room is a nice option as well. Since the dog is a social animal,

he needs to feel a part of his new pack. He needs to see you, hear you, smell you and know that he's not isolated and alone. Most importantly, he should never think of his crate as a punishment area. It must represent a place of security and comfort, never unpleasantness.

His crate should be used not only for sleeping at night but also for napping or resting when there is too much activity going on and

Another of the crate's many benefits is that it is good for travel safety, too. Bring along water for your dog and all of the other amenities he will need, depending on the length of the trip.

you want to keep the puppy out of the way. Most puppies and many older dogs can be crate-trained. Once they are, you may even find that they will seek the comfort of their crates from time to time when they feel the need to get away from the hubbub of family life. When this happens, you'll know you've done a good job of crate-training!

When you begin the training process, place the crate in the area where the dog spends most of his time. Leave the door open and let the dog become accustomed to the crate's being nearby. Placing a dog biscuit just inside the door of the crate will encourage him to reach in and pick up the treat. Little by little, you can place the biscuit farther back in the crate so that

A CLOSER EYE, CLOSE BY
Limiting your puppy's freedom in the house will cut down on the number of accidents he has. Keeping the puppy with you whenever he's not in his crate helps you recognize his signals to go out, thus preventing indoor accidents.

the dog actually has to enter the crate to retrieve the treat. That way, he gets used to the idea that the crate is a good thing and will not harm him.

Just as we raise kids and set their schedules, so must we show the dog when it's time to play, eat, sleep, exercise and even entertain himself. You can see how his rest area then becomes a pivotal part of his adapting to your lifestyle.

It is important that your pup does not feel isolated in his crate. He can still be part of the family's goings-on while comfortably confined for training and safety purposes.

Mom and hungry pups in an ex-pen on a tiled floor with newspapers. These provisions make for easy cleanup, as very young puppies cannot yet venture outside their quarters to relieve themselves.

Establish control as soon as you bring the dog into your home and you'll find that the dog will adjust quickly and easily to you, his new pack leader.

LARGER OPEN REST AREAS
Sometimes, however, there's an adult dog that's adopted into a new home and he can't tolerate being crated. No matter how hard the new owners try to acclimate the dog to a crate, the dog will not accept the confinement. Quite simply, the dog wasn't crate-trained in his previous home, and he can't cope with it now. Thus this dog will need some special consideration to help him develop a new lifestyle with you. Rest assured, however, that with patience and time, you'll find a way to give the dog his very own safe resting place.

The adult dog that cannot be crate-trained will also need a place similar to the puppy's "cubbyhole" that will offer him security yet is close to his new human pack. Setting up a small fenced area in a garage, a storeroom or a basement will not be suitable. These places, though

If using an open resting area rather than a crate, make it a safely enclosed space in which the dog feels at home.

Baby gates are a good way to expand the area to which your pup has access by keeping him gated in a puppy-proofed room.

probably secure enough to contain the dog, would isolate the dog so much that he may suffer the anxieties of isolation frustration. Such conditions can and often do create serious chronic problems of excessive chewing, barking, digging, even voiding in his sleeping quarters. We must never forget that the dog is a social animal and needs to feel a part of his pack at all times.

A suitable rest area can be made in the corner of the kitchen by using baby gates to create his cubby. Baby gates are ideal because they're expandable and made of plastic or nylon mesh, which allows the dog to see all around just as a wire crate would.

Another possibility would be a small bathroom or utility area close to the home's activity center. Again, pet or baby gates can be used to block off a portion of the room to give the dog a resting area while the door remains open so he can watch family activities.

If the dog is past the teething stage (at eight months of age, the molars will come in and there is the chance for some serious chewing at that time), it should be safe to place a large cushion or dog bed in his area. A toy or two will help occupy his time when he must be confined. Even a bowl of water would be acceptable, providing the area isn't so small that the bowl interferes with his bedding.

Again, in acclimating the dog to his new area, placing him in the area and giving him a dog biscuit as a treat can teach the dog that his rest area represents good things. There are some very hard rubber toys on the market that are designed to be used whenever the dog needs to be confined away from his pack. These toys are designed so you can put peanut butter or a dog biscuit inside. The dog will work for hours to retrieve the treat from the toy, and all the while he's learning that it's OK to be alone.

BREED DIFFERENCES

Most pure-bred and mixed-breed dogs effectively can be house-trained in the same way. Some breeds will learn the routine

Whippets and Greyhounds may take more time to house-train, as they can be a bit stubborn and carefree when it comes to discipline.

Sled-dog breeds can exhibit stubbornness and thus present challenges to their owners in house-training.

effortlessly overnight, and others may prove a little stubborn or oblivious. Knowing about your breed's temperament traits can ready you for what lies ahead. A Whippet or Greyhound can be arrogantly single-minded and really aggravate his owners; likewise, a Siberian Husky, American Eskimo or Norwegian Elkhound can exhibit similar hard-headed tendencies. Even so, there are no special tricks to house-training a Golden Retriever versus a Poodle, though owners should realize that certain breeds or kinds of dogs pose special difficulties when trying to establish their toileting routines. The hound breeds, for instance, require a bit more patience, consistency and deodorizers. Beagles, Basset Hounds, Bloodhounds and the coonhound breeds not only have incredible noses but also have a more kennel-oriented mentality. Kennel dogs tend not to be as fastidious as house dogs, so moving a scenthound into your home will require more effort than, say, a Boxer or Pit Bull, especially if the hound was previously not a house dog. Likewise, the nose of a

Scenthounds like the Basset Hound also can be challenging to train, as there aren't many deodorizers that can fool these extra-talented noses!

scenthound is so keen that he can still detect his past indiscretions on your flooring (i.e., piddles and puddles) for a long time. Investigate deodorizers made for cleaning up pet potty accidents and don't be sparing in applying them.

Another type of canine proves to be an exception to the rule, and this is the male toy dog. If the dog is an intact (unneutered) male, he may develop the habit of lifting his leg whenever and wherever he chooses with no obvious regard for your house rules. What's even worse is that the urge to procreate is extremely strong in this little fellow and once he matures, he begins lifting his leg to mark his territory in the house. Of course, this marking behavior is not the same as elimination, but it's still a problem to be dealt with. At first, you won't notice his nasty little habit; thus his undesirable behavior goes on uncorrected. Before long, it becomes a permanent habit that's extremely difficult, if not impossible, to break.

Normal urination is when a dog empties his bladder, usually in one or two times of lifting his leg and passing urine. In contrast, urine marking is done to notify other dogs of his presence and to warn them that he considers a

A small male dog with a territorial bent may be prone to marking behaviors that can frustrate his owners.

particular area as his domain. Marking consists of leg lifting repeatedly and spraying small amounts of urine on upright objects. It does not consist of large quantities of urine at any one time.

What happens is that when he marks his territory, he lifts his leg on anything that's perpendicular to the floor—the corner of a sofa, a chair, the drapes, your bedspread, a doorway. But because he's small and his marking consists of only a few drops of urine, you hardly notice this misdemeanor. It isn't until months go by that the accumulation of dried urine on your furniture begins to create an unpleasant smell in the house.

In the case of a larger dog that lifts his leg indoors, you would notice puddles of urine almost as soon as they appear. In that case, you would correct the dog and insist that he urinate outdoors and not lift his leg indoors. But with a tiny dog, you don't notice until the habit is well established, because two drops of urine do not a puddle make!

To prevent this behavior from ever happening with pet dogs of all breeds and sizes, have the dog

Sometimes males lift their legs to mark and squat to urinate for relief, while others lift their legs every time they urinate. The best way to tell the difference is in the amount of urine expelled.

Further, spaying eliminates the possibility of the female's producing unwanted puppies while also contributing to her becoming a loving, more dedicated companion to her family. In addition, you will never have to cope with her coming in season twice a year.

A dog's daily routine must include times for meals, relief trips and trips outdoors just for recreation.

CREATE A SCHEDULE

You must clearly define the time and place for your dog to relieve himself as soon as you bring him into your home. As for a relief area, establish a place that will become his relief zone, which he'll always use for urinating and defecating. If that area is outdoors, be sure to decide on a place that

neutered. Prevent the dog's body from producing testosterone and you will eliminate his need to mark. Regardless of size, the dog will make a far nicer companion all around. In addition, you will need to control the dog by keeping him within your sight at all times except when he's in his crate or rest area. Eventually he can be trusted to have more and more freedom inside the home as he matures and his relief habits become acceptable.

Incidentally, while we're on the subject of neutering, females should be spayed as well. Both neutering and spaying have important health benefits for dogs.

An important rule with puppy house-training is that what goes in comes out rather quickly.

will be convenient for you to keep clean and for the dog to use in all types of weather.

For example, setting up a relief area at the back corner of a large property would prove impractical in the snow of winter when you and the dog have to trudge out in the snow to reach it. Find a place closer to the house, but not near a patio or walkway, a place that is easy to clean and accessible in all types of weather conditions.

For indoor training, be sure the area you choose will always be available to the dog. If, for example, family members occasionally shut the door to that room, the dog would be locked out of his relief area. A few times

of finding his relief area closed will quickly create a dog that is forced to relieve himself somewhere else in the house.

Depending upon the dog's age, you will need to set up a training schedule that allows the dog reasonable access to his relief area on a regular basis. Very young puppies need to go as often as every one to three hours. At ten weeks of age, a puppy will usually urinate every hour. By the time he's 12 weeks old, he can usually hold his urine for about 2 hours.

Remember too that strenuous activity and napping are usually followed immediately by the need to void. The best guide to learning about when your dog needs to

The activity of a vigorous game of fetch—a favorite of retrievers and many other types of dog—may bring on the need for a potty break.

Do you want to trudge through the snow every time your dog needs to go out? Think of convenience when choosing a relief area, but make sure the spot isn't too close to doors and walkways.

urinate is to realize that he will probably void right after a nap, after a play period, after a meal or whenever you notice him sniffing and turning in circles as if trying to decide upon where he wants to go. Also keep track of his water intake. The best advice for new dog owners is to keep your eye on the dog. It won't take long for you to learn the behavioral signals he gives when he's ready to relieve himself.

Defecating for a dog occurs several times a day but not as frequently as urinating. You must set up a schedule for your dog's relief periods. Depending on your schedule, the puppy's feeding plan and other criteria, you can devise a plan that works for both of you. With a puppy, most

Large-breed owners really appreciate the benefits of a crate-trained, clean house dog; otherwise, they would be dealing with some very big messes.

important is that you are consistent. You can't come home from work at 4 p.m. every day, except Fridays, when your "happy hour" keeps you out until 9 p.m. The dog will adjust to your schedule, but you must keep it the same from day to day, within reason, of course.

Fortunately, the relief schedule for an adult dog is a lot less demanding than that for a puppy. Most adult dogs do well with four or five relief periods a day: when they first get up in the morning, again about midday, before dinner, after they've had their second meal and once again before going to bed.

Never take your dog's piddle or pile for granted. Praise the dog lavishly whenever he voids in the appropriate area. He needs to learn that relieving himself in the correct area pleases you. He'll look forward to your sincere praise when he's done well, and receiving it will encourage him to use that area again.

One final note here: taking your dog outdoors to relieve himself is not the same as taking your dog outdoors for exercise. Most dogs need and enjoy one or two sessions of physical activity a day in the fresh air. A brisk walk, a jog, playing with a favorite toy, catching a flying disk or just strolling leisurely down a quiet street are all activities enjoyed by most dogs, regardless of size.

DEVELOPING FLEXIBILITY

Eventually your dog can become reasonably flexible in his relief schedule. As an adult, he won't need to go as often as when he was a puppy. His bladder and bowel muscles will be stronger and under more control, so he can hold it for longer periods of time. This maturity will often come in handy on many occasions.

For example, in cases of extremely bad weather he can postpone going out for up to several hours until the rain stops or subsides. If you are ill and unable to take him out, he can hold it until another member of the family comes home. If your work schedule changes, the dog can learn a new set of potty times. When traveling with your dog, he can learn to go whenever the opportunity arises and in strange places such as restaurant and motel lawns or parking areas.

Keep in mind that full muscle control comes only with maturity. It cannot be trained into the dog. His body develops at a certain rate in a particular pattern, and nothing you do can change this! Be patient with puppies, young dogs and adult dogs that are making the transition to a new home. With careful planning and understanding, you'll soon have a house-trained dog that's reliable and accepting of when and where to relieve himself.

DOG/OWNER COMMUNICATION

LET'S TALK

Although dogs can't speak to us in a human language, they do communicate with us by their behavior. We learn to recognize their signs and signals, their barks, whines, tail wags and nose rubs, their grunts, grumbles and growls. We apply our theories and principles to the behavior and signs we understand. For example, we recognize the dog's desire to keep his sleeping area

The crate has many uses both in the home and away from home. It's the essential all-around tool for your dog's training, safety and comfort.

clean. We, in turn, take that basic instinct and use the crate to help us house-train the dog. We praise the dog for not voiding in his crate, and he begins to show us by his behavior when he feels the need to eliminate. Then we praise him again. That's communication in action.

However, there's a lot more to this crate thing than simply getting the dog to not relieve himself inside it. The benefits of crate-training reach far into many elements of having a dog in your home. Here are some of them:

- Destructive behavior, such as chewing household items like sofas, chair legs, baseboards, magazines, newspapers, shoes and a myriad of personal items can all be avoided by crate-training.
- Crates are perfect for keeping dogs comfortable and safe during automobile trips. Staying in hotels and motels when you have a dog with you can be much easier if you can crate the dog in your room; further, some establishments do not allow uncrated pets.
- Crate-training your dog can make the trauma of being

Crating the puppy encourages his good habits by preventing him from engaging in destructive behavior such as chewing inappropriate items.

hospitalized much less upsetting to the dog. When a dog is kept at the veterinary clinic for treatment, he will be crated. If a dog has never been crate-trained, he will find being at the clinic even more stressful than he would if he were accustomed to a crate. Stress is the worst thing for a sick dog.

- There are many times in the dog's life when he will seek the peace and quiet of his crate. "Time out" means that he can take a break if there's a lot going on in the home. For example, he can rest without being pestered by young children who want to play with him.
- Finally, a crate is the ideal place in your home for the dog if he is not feeling well. In his own private space, he can sleep and recuperate without being disturbed.

Certainly you're beginning to see how beneficial crate-training is for both you and your dog. It will make all the difference in the world in the dog's transition to your lifestyle—for both of you. When a learning process goes smoothly and rapidly, the experience will be one of pleasure, not frustration and disappointment.

Don't think that an adult dog is easier to train. His muscle control may be developed, but you still need the same consistency that you would with a puppy.

CANINE SIGNS

During this house-training process, your dog will speak to you in many ways, so you'll need to be alert to what he's telling you, especially about his relief needs. For example, when the dog begins to sniff the floor and turn in circles, you can be sure he has to either urinate or defecate or both. That's the moment that you need to get him outdoors quickly.

If he's a puppy, you can pick him up and rush outside to his relief area. If he's an adult, snap on his lead quickly and head outdoors. The dog, whether puppy or adult, should wear his collar and lead while he's in his relief area. That way, he cannot wander off and do his business

anywhere he chooses. You should hold the lead and stand quietly at the edge of his area. Don't talk to the dog, as this will only distract him. Let him concentrate on the business at hand.

Stay only five minutes and no more. If you stay longer than that, he'll figure out that he can keep you outdoors as long as he likes by simply acting as though he could not decide upon a spot in which to eliminate. That's the same reason why you want to go to one area and just stand there. Otherwise, walking around the yard or neighborhood becomes a stroll to the dog and he forgets about relieving himself until he's back in the house again. As he is doing his business, praise him

If your dog doesn't go within the first five or so minutes, return home and try again later. Otherwise, your clever dog will quickly learn that the longer he delays in relieving himself, the longer he will get to stay outside, sniffing and exploring.

Now here's a signal that's hard to miss!

and then, once he is finished, get back indoors quickly so he doesn't learn that sniffing and circling indoors is the ticket to going outside to play.

When you first notice the sniffing and circling signs, you should give him a command that will forever mean "Let's go out." Many people say that exact statement to their dogs. Others ask the question "Do you want to go out?" Some tell the dog to "Go potty." Whatever is a comfortable command for you will be fine for the dog once you establish it as his signal to go out. However, you must be consistent in your verbal language as well as your body language.

Keep in mind that both you and your dog are developing a behavioral language that will be yours for your entire life together. Thus, giving some forethought to the way you physically speak to

the dog will pay big dividends. For example, always putting on his collar and lead as you say "Let's go out" becomes the first sign that he's going outdoors. Then taking him to his relief area is another signal that it's time to eliminate, not exercise or play.

Eventually the dog may add some new behaviors to his repertoire when he wants to tell you that he needs to go out. He may go to the door and sit there, waiting for you to notice him. Or maybe he'll go to the door and bark or just do a little dance. Or sometimes a dog will get his own lead if it's in a place that he can reach. I once had a Poodle that would bring me his lead every time he wanted to go out. No matter where I was in the house, he would find me. I'd look down and there would sit my friend with his lead in his mouth as he waited ever so patiently for me to notice him.

You may not be as lucky as I was to have a dog who's ready to "walk himself," but whatever signs you begin to recognize in

CRATE LIMITATIONS

A dog that is left in his crate too long may develop the habit of voiding in his crate. Once established, that habit is almost impossible to break. Thus, be sure to have someone available to take the dog out at the scheduled times when you can't be home with him.

your dog, be sure to praise him for his effort. As you bend down to hook up his lead, be sure and let him know how happy you are that he signaled his need to you. Remember, dogs want to please you and they're thrilled when you tell them they do. Your happy tone of praise is their pay for good deeds done.

THE CITY DOG

This is the dog that almost never has the opportunity to void on grass or soil. He lives in a world of cement and thus must accustom himself to voiding on this surface. Most cities have dog-walking and pooper-scooper laws. Most of them state that dogs must eliminate in the curb area and not on the sidewalk. Therefore city dogs are programmed to using the area just off the sidewalk below the curb.

When house-training the city puppy, take him down to the curb to do his business and then take him right back indoors. For the first few days, do not take the pup for walks to explore the neighbor-hood. Resist the temptation of showing off your new puppy. By immediately returning inside, you are telling the puppy that going down to the street means it's time to eliminate, not sniff around, wander about the neighborhood or bark at the cars. By the end of the first week, you'll have a dog that automatically relieves himself

when he gets outside, and then you can stroll leisurely. This little trick also simplifies your life on rainy days and Mondays (when you're running late) and on other days when it's blustering cold or snowing. Your well-trained pal will relieve himself right away, at the curb closest to your front stoop, and you won't be ambling down the avenue waiting for him to pick a special tree or favorite plot six blocks upwind.

All puppies squat to urinate, and female dogs continue this behavior as adults. There should be no problem getting your puppy or adult female dog to use the curb area to urinate. Adult male dogs, however, usually lift their legs when they urinate, so you'll

It's not just city dogs that need relief walks... sometimes suburban owners don't have fenced yards, so their dogs must get in the habit of going for walks to relieve themselves on the curbside.

Indoor training is an option for owners of small dogs. Instead of using newspaper, this Silky Terrier is accustomed to going on absorbent pads, available at pet-supply shops just for this purpose.

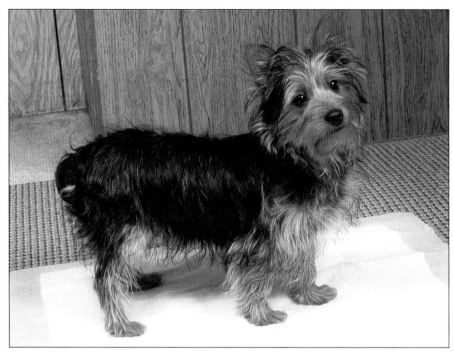

need to be creative when training your macho man to relieve himself in the city. Introduce him to the telephone pole, a fire plug or any large cement markers that are close to where you live. Be considerate and never allow the dog to urinate on trees, cars, mailboxes, plants or shrubbery. And be sure to pick up all feces whenever and wherever your dog defecates. Bring plastic bags or a "poop-scoop" device whenever you take your dog out.

A dog can be acclimated to whatever conditions his environment presents. City dwellers should take their dogs to the dog park or other recreational areas where dogs can enjoy that wonderful suburban commodity known as grass. Dogs naturally take to grass because it's soft, fresh and smells like every dog that's ever pawed at it. This is also helpful when you visit the country so that, when you take him on vacation or visits outside the city, he'll be perfectly comfortable voiding in whatever area you have available to you.

Likewise, the dog that's paper-trained in the house will probably need to learn how to eliminate outdoors too. Going on vacation, visiting friends and family, trips to the vet's office and shopping trips to the pet store are all

A savvy New Yorker, this Cavalier King Charles Spaniel knows how to live the clean life in the city.

occasions when your indoor dog may need to relieve himself outdoors. Exposing the dog to both city and suburban environments will be useful during special times as well.

To make the transition easy for the indoor dog, simply choose

a time when you know that he needs to void. Put on his collar and lead and take him outdoors to a predetermined area. Stand still and allow him time to sniff around and familiarize himself with the area. Because he needs to go, he'll probably relieve himself soon after being placed on the ground. As soon as he does, praise him and bring him back indoors. Repeat this every few days until he becomes accustomed to going on his paper indoors and in a relief area outdoors. Since physical activity stimulates body functions, a brisk walk will also encourage him to relieve himself.

INDOOR TRAINING

When training the little dog to use a potty pad or newspaper indoors, use the same signals that you'd use for outdoor training. Put on his collar and lead. Teach him the same verbal signals that you would use if taking the dog out. If you simply carry him into the room where his relief area is and set him down, he's liable to run around the room and eliminate anywhere he chooses, on or off the paper. You must place him on the papered area.

By standing still next to his area and keeping him on lead so you can control him while he prepares to eliminate, you are teaching him to go on the paper, not any place else. Eventually, as he gets older, you can teach him

LIFT UP YE GATES!

One of the easiest ways to manage your dog in the house is to use regular baby gates to control where the dog is allowed to go. Keeping the dog confined to a certain area of the home or a group of rooms such as the kitchen and family room allows you to monitor the dog and watch for signs of his needing to eliminate. Then getting him outdoors quickly once you recognize his signal reinforces his success in becoming house-trained. Confining the dog also keeps him safe, as you will "dog-proof" the areas to which he has access.

A new puppy should bring joy to the whole family!

Indoor training means paper-training. You will have to take the pup to his relief area with the same consistency and frequency, but the area will be a place indoors that you've chosen rather than a spot outdoors.

to use the paper in other areas of the home or even in other places if you visit friends or family who don't mind his going indoors.

In other words, you've trained him to the paper, not the room. That way, his relief habit will be very flexible and he'll become a good traveler. Just remember to always have him on lead whenever you introduce a new place for elimination, and praise generously when he uses the paper correctly.

STAY-AT-HOME OWNER

If you stay at home most of the time, house-training will be easy for you and the dog because you'll be available for frequent elimination trips. A young puppy will need to go often, sometimes as frequently as every hour if he's 10 to 12 weeks old. As he grows, however, his bowel and bladder muscles mature and he won't feel the need to void as often.

Generally, a puppy needs to relieve himself when he wakes up in the morning, after each meal and drink of water, after every nap, after exercising or vigorous play periods, after an exciting activity such as the arrival of friends or family members and right before bedtime.

Adult dogs usually do well with five or six trips outdoors per day: first thing in the morning, after breakfast, midday, before dinner, after dinner and before

going to bed at night. Many owners, due to their home circumstances or physical limitations, have to accustom their dogs to fewer trips outdoors; these dogs appear to experience no ill effects.

The fact that you are home most of the time means that the dog will be sleeping less and keeping more active just following you around the house. That activity alone will stimulate him and create a need to void more frequently than the dog that spends his days alone.

THE WORKING OWNER

If you are a working owner and gone from the home for many hours each day, you must make arrangements for your dog's needs. For example, you will need to get up earlier in the morning so that you will have time to take the dog out before leaving. Remember that once puppy awakens, he will need to go out immediately. Very young puppies can't hold it for long!

Feed the dog his breakfast very early in the morning. Most young puppies will urinate and defecate during their initial morning trip outdoors. Then they'll do it again immediately after they eat. This is normal and can be expected since you feed the young puppy more often than the older dog. In addition to that, the young puppy eats more per unit of body weight than the adult dog because he's growing at a rapid rate.

Finally, just before you leave the house in the morning, give the puppy one last chance to urinate before you put him in his crate for the day. If at all possible, try to arrange to have someone come in around noontime and take the puppy out. Perhaps a neighbor will be willing to help, since it's a temporary situation. You may be able to come home during your lunch hour and take the puppy out. Or perhaps there's another family member who can drop in for the noontime outing. There are other options as well, such as a professional dog walker or doggie daycare. Investigate these options in your community.

With a very young pup, it's a blessing if the owner is at home during the day, because the owner can spend more time acclimating the pup to the crate, supervising the pup and making frequent trips outdoors.

House-training a dog certainly takes time, effort and dedication, but once your dog is trained, you will be rewarded with a clean, well-mannered companion who fits into your family and home and with whom you love spending time.

Please do not abuse the crate: the puppy can be left in the crate for a few hours, not eight! A three- to four-month-old puppy can last three to four hours; a five- to six-month-old puppy can last about six hours. No youngster should be expected to be confined for longer periods of time.

If you find that puppy has had an accident in his crate, do not scold the puppy (or otherwise punish him). Simply greet the puppy happily and get him outdoors quickly. Your puppy is a bright little animal and can read your moods and tone of voice. Control your aggravation and do not shout (even to yourself) while you're mopping up the pee or poo. This will only stress out your puppy, who's already not having a good time in a dirty crate.

You can clean up the accident after the pup has had a chance to go out. Put the puppy in another room so he doesn't see you cleaning up his crate. That way, he won't think that messing in his crate will bring him extra attention. Just keep him out of sight, say nothing about the accident and proceed with the cleanup. Be assured that, as he gets a bit older, he won't have such frequent needs to go out. He'll be able to hold it until you get home, but be sure to come home immediately after work.

In the case of the adopted adult dog, once he's reliably house-trained he should be able to stay clean and dry during the day while you're at work. Take him out when you first get up in the morning, then again just before you leave for the day. Those two trips will be sufficient to make him comfortable all day. Adult dogs do not need to be crated during the day once their house-training is complete and reliable, though many owners like to restrict them to certain dog-safe rooms by closing doors or setting up baby gates.

Never forget that dogs' actions speak loud and clear. Learn to observe them and understand what your dog's actions are telling you. As you begin to understand his sounds and signs, he will begin to understand your combined words and actions. Once you two get on the same page, you'll have a full and rewarding life together.

To help you reach that goal quickly, we'll address the specific steps in teaching crate-training and house-training. Follow each step carefully and don't jump ahead before you've achieved success with the previous step. Here again, the dog will follow your lead to understand what is and what is not acceptable to you.

Six
Crate-training Steps

"Success breeds success." This adage applies to dogs as much as it does to people. When the dog does something good and you recognize his achievement with praise and happy petting, he will want to do it again. Conversely, if he does something bad and you don't acknowledge his behavior (with either praise or discipline), his desire to repeat it will eventually die because he failed to get your attention.

That's the principle of most

successful dog-training methods. Training out of fear will only produce more fear and eventually will drive the dog away from you. But when you help the dog do something that pleases you and then you congratulate him for doing it, he'll be anxious to do it again. Thus positive motivational training offers the quickest and most reliable results.

That's why the following six steps to crate-train your dog will prove easy for you to housebreak the dog and reward him for understanding what is expected. Remember, most dogs want to please people. When your puppy

Show your pup that you love him by putting in the effort to train him properly.

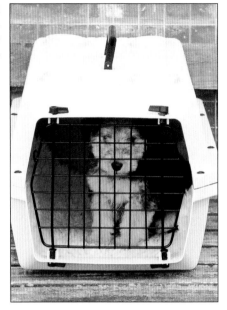

The pup should view the crate as his den, a private retreat all his own.

or adult learns to accept his crate as his special place of security and comfort, you'll have a happy dog.

SIX-STEP PROGRAM FOR PUPPIES

Placing the crate in the room where the puppy will spend most of his time and allowing him to familiarize himself with it will make his first crate experience much easier. Once he sees that the crate is non-threatening, he'll be much more willing to step inside and get that biscuit that you placed in it. Now you can begin the training process.

Step #1: Tell the puppy "It's cubby time!" and place him in the crate with a treat. Shut the

door and stay within his sight just outside the crate. Let him stay there for five minutes while you remain nearby but don't talk to him. At the end of the five minutes, release him and praise lavishly. If he fusses during the five minutes, do not release him. Simply tap on the top of the crate to startle him and when he stops whining momentarily, release him quickly and praise. You want him to realize that he will be released only when he's quiet. Otherwise, he'll think that fussing is his ticket to get out.

Step #2: Repeat Step #1 several times during the first day. Always wait for puppy where he can see you, such as in a nearby chair, watching TV or reading.

Step #3: The next day, place the puppy in his crate as before. Let him stay there for ten minutes this time. Repeat this step several times during the day.

Step #4: Continue to build time in 5-minute increments until the puppy will stay in his crate for 30 minutes with you in the room. Always take him to his relief area after a prolonged (20 minutes or more) period in his crate.

Step #5: Now go back to the beginning and let the puppy stay in his crate for five minutes, but now with you out of the room.

Step #6: Once again, build his crate time in 5-minute increments with you out of the

RUB-A-DUB-DUB
Keeping your dog clean by bathing him regularly encourages him to keep his living area free of urine and feces. If the dog is dirty, the smell of urine and stool on his coat will transfer to the dog's sleeping area and he won't be as fastidious about keeping his bedding clean.

room. When the puppy will stay willingly in his crate (he may even fall asleep) for 30 minutes with you out of the room, he'll be ready to stay in it for several hours at a time.

The primary purpose of crate-training any dog is to achieve house-training success. By letting the dog stay in his crate at sleeping time as well as when you leave him alone, you encourage him to remain clean in his "den." He quickly learns to void outdoors, or on paper in the case of small dogs, while he keeps his sleeping and resting area clean. And as your puppy grows, he'll be able to stay in his crate for longer periods of time because his bladder and bowel muscles are developing.

SIX-STEP PROGRAM FOR ADULT DOGS
Use the same six steps as given for the puppy for crate-training the adult dog. Likely this adult dog has never been in a crate before, so this concept is new to

A pup that likes his crate will be happy in it wherever you take him.

him. You may find that the dog is perfectly fine in the crate while you're in the room with him but that he shows signs of stress or separation anxiety whenever you leave. If that's the case, go back to the beginning and repeat Steps #1 through #4. Be sure not to talk to him while he's in his crate. Just do your own thing while he learns to rest and wait in his crate. Try giving him a toy to play with while he's waiting. A hard rubber toy with a biscuit hidden inside will stimulate his mind while the waiting period passes.

When you release him, be sure to praise him generously. Really make a fuss over him as you tell him what a good dog he is. Take him out to his relief area if he's been crated for more than 20 minutes and again praise him when he urinates.

When crate-training an adult dog that has previously lived outdoors, he may be very reluctant to enter a crate indoors. It's also possible that an adult dog's only experiences in a crate were for isolation or punishment and thus were not pleasant. Your goal is to make crate time happy, pleasant and completely non-threatening. Keeping the crate with its door open in an area where the dog spends time will help the dog become accustomed to seeing it.

Though I don't recommend feeding puppies in their crates, because they can and often do make big messes with their food, you might try feeding the adult dog in his crate. Adults, unlike puppies, don't have the habit of playing with anything and everything that's within their reach. Feeding an adult in his crate will also serve to relieve his anxiety about the crate and make a positive connection with the crate. It becomes a good place to be, since he gets fed there. Keep the door shut while he's eating, but open it and let him out as soon as he finishes his meal. Do not take

Most puppy owners do not feed their youngsters in their crates, as they tend to be messy with their meals.

the bowl out of the crate while the dog's still inside, as this can lead to food-aggressive behavior. A few days of eating in his crate will prepare him to get started on the aforementioned six steps.

If after a few attempts to introduce the dog to his crate he absolutely cannot tolerate it, try an open resting space rather than a crate. You can also feed the dog in his resting area. Even a wire exercise pen placed in a corner of the family room can serve as the adult dog's resting area. However, exercise pens are not suitable for dogs that are fence jumpers or that repeatedly jump or push against the wire sides, because that type of pen is free-standing and he will be able to escape easily.

Once the dog is successful at Step #4, you can move on to Step #5 (five minutes with you out of the room). In the case of the dog in the open resting area, stay

nearby but out of his line of vision. For example, if his space is in the laundry room, don't stay in that room. Go to a nearby room far enough away that he can't see you as you proceed with your own activities during his confinement time.

Some crates open from the top, while others have front and/or side doors. Any opening should be latched securely when closed.

ADDITIONAL TIPS

Of course, you know that crate-training provides safety for you, the dog and your home. When your dog is in his crate and no one is home, he usually sleeps because it's quiet and there is nothing going on around him to incite his curiosity. Chewing on electrical cords, furniture, clothes, shoes and other forbidden items is the recipe for disaster. This behavior is not only costly but also very dangerous. Biting through a

The rest area must be comfortable for the dog, not too big and not too small, and impossible for the dog to escape from. This Poodle seems fine with his cozy little corner.

Trees are favorite marking and sniffing spots of dogs of all ages, though the trees don't like it much.

television wire, for example, can electrocute the dog and start a fire in the house. A crated dog is not able to engage in such destructive and harmful behaviors.

If you have a dog that insists on whining and barking whenever he's in his crate, you must not give in to his tantrums. Never release the dog when he's fussing. Tell him sternly "No! Be quiet!" and bang sharply once or twice on the top of his crate. That should startle him and make him be quiet if only temporarily. As soon as he stops making any noise as a result of your action, say "Good quiet! Good boy! Let's go out!" Then take him to his relief area immediately and praise when he uses it. With this method, you'll be teaching him that only when he's quiet will you take him out of his crate. Of course, if he gives a little happy squeal when he sees you coming to take him out, don't treat that as a nuisance whine. He's just expressing his delight at seeing you and having the sweet smell of freedom in the air.

It is extremely important that you be consistent with the command you use when you want the dog to go into his crate or rest area. If you train properly and enthusiastically, the dog will run to his space when he hears the special word. Many owners commonly use phrases such as "Go to your cubby," "Kennel up" and "Crate time" as commands. Giving the command in a happy tone of voice and with a biscuit in your hand will get your dog's attention and produce a positive response from him within just a few days. Try it, you'll see!

Just remember that your attitude about whatever you train your dog to do will be reflected in his response to your verbal and physical signals. A positive response from you when you release him from his space will also reinforce his acceptance of his crate or resting area. Praising him for being a good dog will help him develop a willing attitude about his special place of comfort and safety.

Don't let house-training drive you up a tree! It's not so bad if you take the time to do it right.

When planning separate trips for exercise and relief, consider your individual dog's activity level. The Dalmatian is a very energetic breed and will need plenty of time for daily exercise in order to be happy.

CREATING A SCHEDULE

THE BEST SCHEDULE FOR YOU
Are you a creature of habit, or are you a free spirit? Your dog is the original creature of habit, and he thrives on structure and regularity. Setting up the ideal schedule for his exercise and elimination will take a little planning. You want to coordinate the best daily schedule that works for you and your dog so that you both are satisfied and comfortable. Once you and the dog have established a regular routine, you will know precisely when to tend to your dog and his needs.

Keep in mind that your puppy's schedule will change as he grows; a young pup's schedule is more demanding. When the pup's bladder and bowel muscles develop, he'll have more control over his elimination habits. He won't need to urinate as often, and he'll probably develop a twice-a-day stool schedule. First we will propose a few routines for puppies from 8 to 20 weeks of age. Then we will recommend a schedule to meet the needs of the older puppy that's almost ready to assume an adult schedule.

In establishing the schedule, you must take into account your own time commitments as well as your puppy's needs. If you live with a spouse or partner who works different hours, you have the advantage of his or her help; likewise, family members can pitch in to help out with house-training the pup. Alternatively, if you live alone, there is more to consider. For example, perhaps you work days and are away from the house for many hours each day. Maybe you work nights and you're home during the day. Or

Whether training indoors or outdoors, you will have to place the puppy in his given relief area until he learns to go there on his own. You always want to stay close by to be sure he doesn't stray from the chosen spot.

All members of the family should participate in the dog's care and be part of the daily routine.

you may not work outside the home at all. That means you'll have more time and more flexibility to create a routine for your puppy.

If you're home all day and you're training an adopted adult dog, you'll find his needs much different from those of a three-month-old puppy. He'll also require more physical exercise in the form of longer walks. That, however, is a good thing because it will give you the opportunity to get out with him and enjoy fresh air along with brisk walks or some stimulating jogging. Either way, the adult dog's physical requirements will be good for both of you. Have you ever noticed that fit and healthy people typically own fit and healthy dogs? Not only do active dog owners look better and

feel better, they also meet lots of other nice dog owners who are walking their dogs around the neighborhood, playing in the park or even window shopping on Main Street.

Exercise and socialization are good things for dogs and their people. Getting outdoors with your dog on a regular basis is a marvelous way to develop new friends or even spark a new romance. For many people, a whole new world opens up when they add a dog to their lives. Going to the bank, the gas station or the pet-supply store is a lot more interesting and fun when you take the dog along, and it's great socialization for him, too.

Before we get into the dog's exercise schedule, consider your own activity schedule, then plan

During the house-training process, dogs can be a lot like babies, requiring constant supervision and attention to their needs...and causing their owners to forgo some sleep!

This Aussie pup knows the purpose of this walk and gets right to business.

when you'll be available to take the dog outdoors for elimination. During the house-training period, be consistent with your schedule so the dog quickly learns when he'll be going outdoors to his relief area. Despite the fact that your dog can not tell time by a clock (which saves you money on buying him a watch or alarm clock!), in just a short time he'll know his going-out times. His excited behavior and little whimpers and squeals will remind you that he knows it's time to go out.

As the dog matures and becomes accustomed to living with you, he can also learn to be flexible in his schedule, too. But for now, be sure to stick to the training plan until the dog is physically mature and reliable in the house.

Just like infants and toddlers, young puppies need to eliminate more frequently than their adult counterparts. If you get your puppy at eight weeks of age, he'll need to go out about every hour. If the puppy is 12 weeks of age, he can probably hold it for two hours unless he's actively playing or running around, in which case he'll need to eliminate as soon as he settles down. By 16 to 20 weeks of age, he will normally be able to control his bladder for several hours. The exception, of course, would again be periods of activity. By this age, however, he'll also begin to give clear behavioral

A puppy owner is shaping his new charge's overall behavior, not just his toileting habits. Directing the pup's chewing onto proper items is a big part of early training.

Toddlers and pups
have lots in
common!

IF YOU CAN'T BEAT 'EM, FEED 'EM

You may be able to break your dog's habit of eliminating in an undesirable location by feeding him there. For example, if he voids in his crate, make sure his crate is not too big for his size and feed him in it. That way, he associates eating with his crate and he'll likely not use the crate for elimination. Or, if your dog is piddling on your dining room rug, place his dinner bowl on the spot. Once he's accepted the place as his eating area, he may stop peeing there.

signs of needing to urinate. Circling or moving around as if he is searching for something, sitting at the door, soft whining sounds and panting are all signals that he feels the need to eliminate.

In all of these cases, it will be your job to pay attention to the dog, anticipate his needs before accidents happen, and get him outdoors in time for him to be successful. If you give the dog too much freedom in the house and fail to observe his signaling behavior, you'll be setting up the dog to fail. Enough failures and the house-training program will not produce the clean, well-mannered pet you want.

In short, what you do and the way you do it will spell success or failure in house-training your puppy. Evaluate your activity schedule and prepare to meet the puppy's needs within the scope of your own personal availability. Once you do that, you can move on to create a potty and exercise program for your dog. Some trips outdoors will be "strictly business," while others will allow the pup some free time in the yard or on-lead walking after he's relieved himself.

Let's mention here that owners of large-breed puppies (or mixed-breed pups with paws the size of oven mitts) should be wary of allowing their puppies to exercise too vigorously. Such pups with lots of growing to do should be restricted from any kind of activity that can stress their developing ligaments and muscles. Permanent skeletal damage can and will occur from this kind of activity, and owners must not allow their pups to roughhouse, run at break-neck (or break-*leg*) speed, climb on top of tables or platforms or jump from furniture or steps. Keep these puppies on-lead when exercising so you can control their activity. Once they are 12 months old, you can lift these activity restrictions and not worry so much about potential orthopedic injuries. Up until the dog is one year of age, though, you're in charge of the playground.

PROPOSED PUPPY SCHEDULES

Let's look at some suggested relief time schedules for puppies of various ages. These time frames are not written in stone. Always be flexible enough to adapt your potty and exercise times to satisfy both you and your dog.

OWNER AT HOME ALL DAY

Puppy age between 8 and 14 weeks

- When puppy awakens in the morning
- After breakfast
- Mid-morning
- Before noon meal
- After noon meal
- Mid-afternoon
- Before dinner
- After dinner

PET-SITTERS FOR RENT

In addition to doggie daycare centers, your veterinary office or grooming shop may offer a dog-sitting service where you can leave your dog for the day while you're at work. In the case of a puppy, most dog-sitters will continue his house-training regimen and get him outdoors often while he's there. Pet-sitting services are listed in your local phone directory; also ask your vet to recommend a good one.

- One to two hours later, depending on puppy's activity
- At bedtime

OWNER WORKS DURING THE DAY
Puppy age between 8 and 14 weeks of age
- When puppy awakens in the morning
- After breakfast
- Before noon meal
- After noon meal
- As soon as you get home
- Before evening meal

Crate-training should begin with the puppy starting on the very first day that you bring him home.

- After evening meal
- During evening
- At bedtime

A very young puppy will need a noon meal, and he'll need to go out before and after his lunch. If you can't get home at lunchtime, someone else will need to take care of the puppy at noontime. Therefore you'll need to arrange help from a friend, a neighbor, a family member or a dog-sitter who can stop by your place and care for the puppy during lunch hour.

A new popular option for dog owners is doggie daycare, a true blessing for busy dog owners who work 9-to-5 days. If your puppy meets the basic socialization requirements, he will be accepted into the daycare center. You will bring the puppy to the center every morning on your way to work and then pick him up on your way home in the evening. During the day, he will be taken outdoors frequently and also given his midday meal according to your directions. You may or may not be required to provide his particular brand of food, but the daycare employees will gladly feed him at lunchtime. Depending on the facility, there may be playtime with other puppies, kindergarten puppy classes, grooming, veterinary care and much more available to your puppy.

Generally the cost for this type of service is quite affordable. Most such centers offer a weekly rate for dogs that spend every weekday there. When shopping for a good daycare center, you will need to visit the facility with your puppy. The quality establishments will evaluate you and your dog just as you will evaluate their services. You should take note of the following things: Is the place clean? Do the dogs seem to get along well together? Are the employees kind and competent? Are the puppies and very young dogs kept separately from the large dogs? It is wise to speak to other dog owners who use the center and get their opinions. Your veterinarian may also be familiar with the center and its services.

OWNER WORKS NIGHTS

This situation calls for a reverse of the first scenario. The puppy will be sleeping all night, so his elimination needs will be minimal. A very young puppy may need to go out at least once during the

TOO LITTLE TOO WET

Puppies under six months of age are unlikely to be consistent in giving you relief signals. Like very young children, by the time they realize they need to void, it's usually too late to let you know. Therefore, to prevent accidents, all family members must cooperate in getting the puppy out to his relief area often until he begins to signal his elimination needs.

night or early morning hours before you get home. Fortunately, by the time the puppy is 12 weeks old he should be able to sleep through the night in his crate. For the young puppy, you'll need to have someone available to take him out when he awakens and whimpers or fusses, indicating his need to urinate. As soon as he voids, he should be returned to his crate immediately without a lot of conversation or attention, as that will make him think it's time to get up when, in fact, it's still the middle of the night. Just put him back in his crate and turn out the light; he'll settle down again quickly.

During the day, you'll be home to take him out when he needs to go. His frequent need to urinate will subside soon, so you'll have only a few weeks during which your normal sleep pattern will be broken into shorter periods.

Many crate-trained adults wander in and out of their crates even when their owners are at home, choosing to spend some quiet time in their own dens.

OWNER WORKS PART-TIME

Here again, adjustments will need to be made in order to satisfy the dog's needs as well as your work schedule. If your work requires you to be away from home for extended periods of time such as more than four hours, you'll need some assistance for a while. Puppy daycare could be the answer, a neighbor or family member may be able to fill in when you're away, a dog-walker could stroll into your life for a while or perhaps you could work for shorter periods of time several days a week.

Evaluate your schedule and balance that with the puppy's needs and you'll arrive at a workable solution to the process of house-training. Keep in mind that the puppy's needs will change almost weekly as his little body

matures. As he grows and matures, he's also learning to adapt to you and your lifestyle so that one day the two of you will have a routine that runs like clockwork!

THE OLDER PUPPY

As your puppy grows, his elimination needs change, too. For example, the 12-week-old puppy will probably need to relieve himself every two hours rather than every hour. As he reaches 16 to 20 weeks of age, he'll be able to hold his urine for three to four hours because his bladder muscles are reaching full maturity.

Those muscles, however, won't be fully developed until he's six months old. His bowel muscles will also reach maturity about the same time, meaning that his urgency to pass stool will be better controlled. In addition, his feeding schedule will change from three meals a day to two, thereby reducing the frequency of his needing to eliminate.

THE ADULT DOG'S SCHEDULE

Now let's look at basic schedules for the adult, remembering again to adapt the suggested times to suit your individual situation.

OWNER AT HOME ALL DAY

- Upon waking in the morning
- Mid-morning
- Noontime if possible for elimination and 15 or 20 minutes of exercise

Owners of toy dogs must realize that such small dogs have small bodies that tend to pass waste more quickly.

A dog whose owner works all day will need to go out for a relief trip immediately upon his owner's return home and will certainly appreciate a longer walk to stretch his legs and spend time with the owner he loves.

Once he knows the routine, a dog will race to his spot in the yard when it's time to "go."

- Mid-afternoon
- After evening meal
- Bedtime

OWNER WORKS FULL-TIME
- Upon waking in the morning
- Just before you leave for work
- As soon as you return home in the afternoon (include a brisk exercise walk)
- After evening meal
- Bedtime

CHOOSING AN OUTDOOR RELIEF AREA
In real estate or relief area, think location, location, location. One of the keys to house-training success is choosing a designated relief area before you begin the training process. Once the dog realizes that he is always taken to the same area and he's praised lavishly for eliminating there, he begins to associate that area with the act of voiding.

Now let's think about the surface, which is an important consideration for the dog. Most owners train their dogs to eliminate on grass, that wonderfully regenerative, soft and good-smelling ground covering that suburban owners mow, seed, fertilize and water. As long as owners maintain their lawns, keep them green and make sure they are free of harmful pesticides and other chemicals, grass is the perfect surface for dogs. In the suburbs, it's everywhere; in the cities, it's not. Other options include gravel, dirt, sand and cement. Cement is the second-best choice for owners, since it's easily maintainable and doesn't turn yellow or need fertilizer. Gravel can be hard on dogs' feet, and small gravel is often swallowed by dogs. Dirt and sand are messy, attract stray cats and turn into mud in the rain.

Ideally the area should be close to the home yet out of the direct path of people coming and going into the home. In addition, inclement weather makes taking the dog to a distant area inconvenient for dog and owner, so keep it close and removed from foot traffic. Furthermore, in areas where snow falls in winter, trudging through the snow to a relief area is definitely something you and the dog won't want to do.

Eventually, when the dog matures and becomes accustomed to his relief schedule, you can introduce him to other areas for relief that may be away from the home. Such locations as a dog park, a vacant lot or a suburban roadside can all be used for elimination purposes.

However, it is essential that you pick up after your dog each and every time he passes stool. Picking up feces in your own yard should be done at least every other day, if not every day. Picking up every time he goes away from home is not only considerate on your part but also essential to keeping the neighborhood clean and free of dog droppings. In many towns, it's the law.

CONSISTENCY

Keeping the relief schedule consistent is extremely important in the house-training process. Every member of the family must adhere to the dog's relief times. This initial schedule will not necessarily be the dog's schedule for life. It only means that during the learning process there must be a rigid timetable in order for the dog to know the difference between relieving himself on schedule and eliminating whenever and wherever he chooses. Again, it's structure that matters.

Once the dog accepts the rules for being house-trained and his body is capable of controlling the bladder and bowels, adjustments toward a less demanding routine can be made. However, this will take a little time, and the owner must use praise and patience to reach that point.

My own dog, an adult Toy Poodle, has a "wait range" of

A safe doggie door is one that allows your dog, and only your dog, access to the fenced yard and then back inside as he chooses. This does not replace time spent with your dog, though.

Bringing home a new puppy is such an exciting time for a family. The rewards of a canine companion far outweigh the work that goes into the pup's training.

about two hours. That means she can wait up to an extra two hours beyond her normal time to go out without having an accident. There are times when I just can't get home at my normal hour, so her ability to wait is very helpful for both of us—no accidents in the house and she doesn't wet her bed. However, you eventually arrange your lifestyle to satisfy your dog's physical needs, and your dog can learn to adapt his physical needs in special circumstances, so you'll be set with a program that works well for both of you. And having a dog with good bathroom habits will make life even more wonderful for you and your dog. In no time, you'll find that your little puppy grows into a consistent adult, and then in what seems like just as little time he becomes a not-so-consistent senior. Your life adjusts to this, too.

HOUSE-TRAINING ACCIDENTS

What would cause a supposedly house-trained dog to have accidents in the house?

Answer: There are many possibilities. There are, however, just as many things you can do to help the dog get over the accident syndrome. But before we consider the cause of the accidents, it's important that the dog be examined by your veterinarian to rule out any physical problem, such as a bladder infection, as the cause of the accidents. One thing is certain—punishing the dog for having an accident in the house will not solve the problem and may, in fact, increase the probability that it will happen again.

How so, you ask? Well, creating an accident in the house brought attention from you. The dog, on the other hand, is experi-

While it can be difficult to conceal an accident from a Basset Hound's keen nose, his scenting instinct also works in your favor, as it won't take him long to learn where his relief spot is located.

A dog's diet—his feeding schedule as well as the quality of the food he eats—plays a large role in his potty habits.

encing some sort of a problem with which he cannot cope, so he expresses his frustration by urinating or defecating in the house. In turn, you reacted and the attention from you helped to ease his emotional suffering temporarily. Thus, he reasons, if wetting the floor made you notice him, then doing it again will win him more of your attention.

And so the scenario escalates. He voids in the house. You respond. He receives your attention. He doesn't like the scolding, but having you notice him in any manner is better than not being noticed at all, so he does it again. Rather than respond to his accident, let's consider what may be causing the problem.

Identifying the cause and altering the dog's response to it will eventually correct the situation. Diet, health problems, emotional upsets, family dynamics and unusual happenings in the home are just some of the major causes of accidents in the house. In most of these cases, there are simple solutions that you can implement to correct the problem. With the exception of inherited health problems, the owner can take steps to help the dog overcome his difficulties.

DIET ISSUES

What your dog eats is directly related to his elimination process. Poor- or marginal-quality food is probably the number-one cause of excessive and overly frequent voiding. Furthermore, it can, and often does, cause severe cases of diarrhea.

In addition, when a dog swallows non-edible material his digestive system gets thrown into chaos. His body tries to pass the matter, so his intestinal tract produces extra fluids, thus creating diarrhea.

In the case of poor-quality food, his body cannot assimilate the excessive amount of fillers used to pump up the quantity of food in the bag. For example, there's a big difference between digestible protein and non-digestible protein, the latter of which is frequently found in poor-quality food. And his body knows the difference.

To prevent digestive problems, consult your veterinarian for suggestions about types, brands and amounts of good-quality dog food. Supermarket shelves are filled with an abundance of brands and types of dog food. Knowing which are best

Monitor the safety and condition of your pup's toys. You don't want pup to chew and ingest a piece of a toy, as it could cause him digestive distress or worse.

for your dog involves consideration of his breed, sex, age, weight, lifestyle and health condition. Your dog's doctor is obviously the best person to assess the matter and guide you appropriately in establishing a healthful feeding program, whether you have a puppy or an adult.

DIARRHEA

The causes of diarrhea are many, some obvious, others not. One thing is for sure, however: diarrhea left unchecked can cause severe dehydration and may even be life-threatening to your dog. Never ignore the signs of intestinal trouble.

Feeding the dog commercial food that disagrees with him can cause diarrhea. Be aware of which brand of food you're feeding and

Water keeps a dog's body properly hydrated and is as important to his health as a good-quality diet.

its effect on the dog's digestive system. In addition, diarrhea can occur if you change the dog's diet abruptly. Instead, wean him onto the new food slowly. Firm stool indicates no problem, but loose stool can be a cause for concern and you'll need to discover the reason for it. It can also occur if the dog swallows non-food material.

Let's say you catch your dog chewing on a piece of aluminum foil that he stole out of the trash. Chances are, he swallowed some of it and he needs to be watched carefully. If the piece was small and passes through his digestive system easily, he won't have a problem. If, however, the piece was large and/or does not move smoothly through his system, he will probably get diarrhea and need medical attention. To be safe, you should contact your veterinarian as soon as you discover the fact that the dog has ingested foreign material. The doctor will advise you appropriately. Follow his directions and be alert for potential trouble.

Dogs, especially puppies, are like little children. They put everything that isn't tied down into their mouths. Retrievers are famous for swallowing stones and sticks. Many breeds of dogs, especially the terriers, dedicate themselves to chewing up every toy you give them. Most puppies grab tissues, toilet paper and paper napkins at every opportunity. They run around the house with their prizes hanging from their mouths and frequently swallow them just as you go to take away these treasures.

I don't know of any cases of paper products clogging up the intestines of dogs, but I do know of many dogs that suffered major surgery to remove hard objects such as coins, stones and children's toys. Whatever the situation, consulting your veterinarian is the best way to go when you're concerned about your dog's swallowing anything other than his regular food. In many of these cases, diarrhea is the first symptom that points to major trouble. The wise owner heeds the warning sign.

BOARDING
There are times in life when you must go away and leave your dog behind. Those are the times when boarding the dog in a reputable facility is necessary. Many veterinary clinics offer boarding to their clients, though this is often only available for smaller dogs. There are also many fine boarding kennels that offer individualized attention to each boarder. Puppies, for example, get lots of socializing, extra meals according to the owner's instructions and extra times to go out because they're not yet fully house-trained.

You might ask your breeder if he offers boarding services, as both you and your dog are already familiar with him and know what a good dog person he is.

When the owner returns and brings his dog home again, sometimes the dog acts as if he was never house-trained at all. He has accidents in the house or relieves himself at new and unusual times, such as at 3 a.m. even though he was sleeping through the night before he went to the boarding kennel. You wonder, "What in the world has happened to my dog?"

Only when he's a well-matured adult and accustomed to being boarded from time to time will he be able to handle the switch from home to kennel without acting as if he were never trained at all. It takes many months for the dog to learn the routines of kennel life versus home life and respond appropriately to both situations. This problem is solvable but requires a great deal of owner patience.

When you bring the dog home from the kennel, treat him as if he were a brand-new puppy just arriving in your home for the first time. Keep him under your watchful eye, take him out to his relief area frequently and praise whenever he voids there. Be sure to keep him in his crate when you can't be with him so he doesn't sneak off and relieve himself in another room of the house. Remember, you want success, not failure, with this retraining procedure.

It won't take long at all. The dog will soon remember the old

Instead of boarding, you may choose to bring your dogs along. This English Setter pair is traveling safely and in comfort, with cushiony dog beds in their own partitioned section of the vehicle.

routine and the house rules he lived by before he went to the kennel. It may take a day or two or it may require several days of retraining on your part, but the dog will recall his old habits and soon you'll be back to where you both were before you had to board your dog. Just remember—*patience* and *praise*. Those are the keys to a fast return to normal.

FAMILY CONFLICTS

Disagreements within a family are normal, but when arguments erupt, your dog will probably become emotionally upset. He hears the loud irritated voices of his pack members. He sees the angry looks on their faces. He hears the slamming doors. He becomes worried and fearful because he doesn't understand what has suddenly come over his normally loving family. Of course, his normal response is, "What did they find now? Where can I hide?"

The ensuing emotional stress he experiences may lead to digestive upset, ultimately developing into a case of diarrhea. Like human beings, dogs have emotions, too, but they don't have the ability to express them productively. Therefore, acting out their worries through inappropriate behavior and/or experiencing physical upsets are the ways they have of handling their traumas.

To prevent trauma and stress in the dog during times of conflict within the home, confine the dog to an area away from the scene. (This is, admittedly, difficult to plan, so if you're the instigator of the ensuing row, give little Sammy a bone before the brawl begins.) Put the dog in his crate, let him go out into the yard (providing it's fenced in) or confine him to a separate room with a fun toy until tempers cool down and peace is restored.

FAMILY MEMBER AWAY
Sometimes when a family member goes away, the family dog begins to worry about what happened to him. Did he leave me forever? Where is he? Will he come back to me? Who will take his place in our pack?

We don't know for sure, but we can guess by the dog's behavior that he notices the person's absence and is reacting to it. If the missing person was one of the pack leaders, a husband or wife, for example, the dog is usually more concerned than if the absentee is one of the children in the family. If the adults are present, he feels that his leaders are still here and taking care of him.

Whatever the case, physical upset can be prevented by having the remaining family members give a bit more attention to the dog to take up the slack of the missing member. This might mean a little longer walk, an extra session of play or a new fetching game, something to capture and keep the dog's attention rather than allowing him to dwell on the mystery of the missing family member. Mental and physical stimulation are the perfect preventions for all manner of problems that your dog can experience in times of stress.

HOUSEGUESTS
In the case of houseguests, the dog reacts to a change of household

A dog should be comfortable in his home and as part of his human pack. A happy family means a happy dog!

You can't misread the look of a fearful pup.

Part of pup's early socialization is acclimating him to being handled, held and petted so that he always welcomes this type of attention.

it makes more sense for the dog's family to only invite over dog people, so that the dog can be the center of attention (which won't lead to any potty accidents at all!). Unfortunately, as the case may be, your in-laws or your husband's friends from college are never dog people!

Physical stress can be avoided by consciously setting aside some special time for the dog to receive the attention he enjoys. Regardless of their prejudices, desires or allergies, encourage the guests to give the dog some attention in the form of short play sessions or just plain moments of affection. Giving the dog something useful to do can provide a substitute for his normal interaction with you. Teach him to bring you his leash when it's time to go out. Teach him to "speak" and then have him speak at the door when he feels the need to eliminate. Have him bring you his toy so you can throw it for him to fetch.

Your own imagination can suggest dozens of activities that you can teach your dog. Keep him stimulated while he learns that having houseguests is really an exciting happening rather than something that deprives him of his normal place in the household.

dynamics. Houseguests tend to take attention away from the dog and onto themselves, especially if the houseguests aren't "dog people." The host family is kept busy seeing that the guests have all the comforts they need as well as providing activities to entertain their visitors. In the meantime, the dog is often left to entertain himself while his pack members focus on the company. Of course,

NEW HOME
Now here's a real cause for concern for any dog. Let's say he's

lived with you for several years in the same home. Circumstances create the need for you to move to a new location and you're expecting to take Max with you. Unfortunately, you can't explain the move to your dog. You take him along to the new home and hope he'll make a comfortable adjustment to it.

Many dogs accept the new home easily when they see you there, too. They recognize the familiar scent of you, other family members and your belongings, including clothing, furniture and household items that he knows are yours. Owners who have traveled with their dogs, doing things like staying in motels or visiting family members for weekends, will have dogs who adjust better to new environments.

Other dogs have a difficult time making the adjustment. Despite the familiarity of scents and your personal belongings, the dog worries about the new surroundings. The house is different, his resting area has moved, the yard smells new, the neighborhood is not the same, even his exercise schedule may change due to a new lifestyle. There are strange new people and pets everywhere he goes, and the whole affair causes him grave concern.

Since there's no way for you to explain the situation to your

dog, you must find ways to show him that things are still fine and the new home is a good place to be. Be sure to bring his familiar bed to the new home. Don't wash it before the move or buy him a new one. He'll find comfort in the scents of his familiar bed, which remind him of the old house, and soon the smells of the new home will be familiar, too. Place his bed in an area representing the heart

Moving to a new home means sticking to the old routine. Keeping things as familiar as possible for the dog in a new place will help him make the transition more easily.

Don't get a new dog bed for the new home. The dog's familiar bed will be a comforting oasis for him in the midst of the confusion of being somewhere new.

of the home where he can see and hear all the activity of his pack members. His food and water bowls should be in a similar location to where they were before. A corner of the kitchen is probably the most popular place for most dog bowls.

Don't introduce your dog to the whole neighborhood right away. Let him become familiar with his yard and the immediate surrounding areas first, then branch out as he begins to show his acceptance of his yard and nearby areas. Remember, he'll need to accustom himself to the scents and markings of all of the dogs in this new area. He'll also need to discover favorite new relief areas, too. That's always great fun!

As the dog begins to familiarize himself with the new home environment, he'll have fewer accidents in the house. You can speed up this process by doing what you did when he was first being house-trained. You can praise lavishly when he urinates and defecates outdoors. You can show him how pleased you are when he indicates his need to relieve himself. And finally, you can help him accept his new home by being consistent with the old familiar commands and phrases he recognizes from his earlier home.

NEW BABY

Long before a new baby arrives on the scene, the dog can be introduced to the idea of another family member by familiarizing him with the crib, baby carriage, baby clothes and all the trappings of an infant. Take a doll and treat it like a real baby. Pretend to feed it, bathe it, cuddle it. As the dog watches and investigates your new behaviors, keep recognizing the dog as well.

When you put the doll in the crib, utilize that pretend nap time to interact with the dog. Take him for a walk, play a game with him, brush him, cuddle him, give him the attention that he's become accustomed to. Then, when it's time to turn your attention to the "baby" again, the dog will not feel left out and jealous of the affection you give the child.

When the real baby arrives, the dog will be very curious about this new and often noisy, smelly, demanding "thing" you've brought home with you. Introduce the dog to the baby with soft, loving words while petting him as he sniffs the baby. Make sure the dog knows he's very much loved by his family. Show the dog right from the beginning that the newest family member is a good thing because it brings him, the dog, all kinds of extra attention and affection. Then, by the time the baby is a toddler, the dog will probably look upon the child as his baby, too.

One very important word of caution here: never leave a dog (of any size or age) and a child alone together in the same room. Be sure there is always an adult with the child when any pet is present.

NEW SECOND PET

Thinking about getting another dog? A cat? A bird? A gerbil? Obviously the addition of a new pet will cause your dog some concern. Be assured that no matter how casual you try to be

about another pet, your dog will take notice and react to it.

Some dogs are only mildly curious about a new pet, no matter what the species. Others take offense and treat the pet as an intruder that requires prompt eviction. Regardless of how your dog views the new pet, you must be prepared to help the dog accept the pet.

A kitten is usually more easily accepted than an adult cat. Like most animals, dogs seem to know the difference between babies and adults of all species. Just as you let the dog know how important he is to you when you introduced a new baby, you must repeat the same scenario with a new pet.

A new dog, whether puppy or adult, will demand your attention, but be sure to involve the first dog in the new pet's adjustment as well. The new pet should have his own bed (crate) and feeding bowls. He should be supervised at

A new baby can be a source of stress for the family dog, as he suddenly wonders why he's no longer the center of attention.

The German Shepherd Dog is a loyal working breed that often takes on the role of protector over his family's young ones.

Turtles have the advantage of hard shells to protect them from a pup's advances, but it's always essential to supervise interactions between pets to make sure that they go smoothly and safely.

all times and the two dogs should not be left alone until they've adjusted to one another. Some dogs will take several days to adjust to each other. Some may take even longer. But do not leave the two dogs unsupervised until you're sure they will get along well together. You can help speed up this process by giving lots of attention to the first dog while

helping the new one acclimate himself to your home and routine.

If you are considering adding a rodent to your house, or even a rabbit, you must be very careful. Most dogs, not just the terriers and sighthounds, view small furry things as prey. When a gerbil or a rabbit scampers across the kitchen floor, it is the dog's natural instinct to hunt it down and kill

it. You cannot erase a trait that's been ingrained for thousands of years, so don't even try. Keep the critter in its cage, away from the dog's eyes, nose and teeth. After a period of adjustment, gentle introductions and lots of sweet talking, your dog may accept your hamster or guinea pig, but never leave the two alone together. Never! Realize that if you own a terrier-type dog, a Greyhound or any other breed that hunts small animals, you would be better off leaving that cage of flying squirrels and fancy rats at the pet shop. A puddle of piddle would be the least of your problems in your suddenly calamitous home!

In the case of a new bird, the bird cage must be placed in a safe location away from drafts and away from the dog's reach in case he decides to knock over the cage to investigate the bird. Since birds are frequently frightened by new surroundings, keep the bird caged for at least several days until he begins to relax in his new environment.

If the bird is a parrot or parakeet, get it used to you before you introduce it to the dog. Have it sit on your hand or an open perch and develop a daily routine wherein you interact with it without interference from the dog. Once the bird is accustomed to being out of the cage, you can put the collar and leash on the dog and bring him into the room while the bird is sitting outside the cage.

Approach the bird slowly and make sure the dog does not lunge at the bird or bark at it. Keep the

Many dogs and cats share a home peacefully, such as this Dachshund and his feline companion.

This Bull Terrier is quite interested in a furry little friend. Owners must always be careful about introducing small-mammal pets to their dogs. These types of animals should never be left alone with a dog; even if they do get along well, accidents can happen.

A Golden Retriever pup is probably not this bird's idea of a special delivery!

COPY PUP

Did you know that dogs teach each other? Often an older dog in a home will help to house-train a new puppy just by observation. When the puppy sees the dog eliminate outdoors or on a paper indoors, the puppy will likely copy that behavior. Conversely, puppies readily copy the undesirable behavior habits of older dogs, too. Therefore you will need to use every effort to prevent your new puppy from seeing the older dog's undesirable behavior and praise the puppy when it behaves desirably. For example, if your older dog urinates in a flower bed, be sure to keep your puppy from going near that area. Confine his relief habits to the place you want him to use for elimination.

that is, birds that have been shot. In the home, this translates to your Golden Retriever's unwittingly mangling your cockatiel when he leaps into the air to retrieve it. You will have your hands full if you decide to add a feathered wonder to the home of one of these sporting dogs.

In all of these cases, most dogs can adjust to a second pet without feeling as though they are no longer loved and important members of their pack. It simply takes some patience and effort on your part to make it happen. Use common sense, be positive in your attitude about the newcomer and give the two animals time to adjust to each other.

dog under control as the bird and dog begin to get used to each other. Little by little, you can allow the dog to be in the room with the bird as long as you are supervising both animals. Never leave the bird alone with the dog. A brief moment in which the bird exercises his wings can alarm the dog and incite him to attack the bird.

Just a note here about those dogs known as "bird dogs": these dogs do not *like* birds, they *love* them. They will grab them and mouth them and carry them. The problem is that these dogs are usually picking up felled birds—

The retriever breeds are bird dogs at heart, whether used in the field or not. Their desire to retrieve birds makes them a poor choice for a home with pet birds.

STEALING STOOL

If you own a cat and keep her litterbox where your dog can get to it, the dog will probably eat the cat's stool. Most dogs love cat litterbox droppings, so find a place to keep the litterbox well away from the dog. Placing the cat litterbox on top of a dryer or in a tub (not a shower) helps to keep the dog away from the litterbox.

POOR HEALTH AND MANAGEMENT

House accidents frequently occur when the dog is in poor health. A stomach upset, a virus, a painful injury and a low-grade infection are just some of the reasons why normally clean dogs have accidents in the house. In all of these cases, your veterinarian should supervise the dog's recovery. Doctoring your own dog can be dangerous and sometimes life-threatening to your dog, so see your dog's doctor for help.

Managing your dog properly is just good animal husbandry. Keeping a dog fit, happy and healthy is the best way to have a great companion. One of the major causes of poor health is an inappropriate feeding regimen. Unlike humans, dogs cannot tolerate things like sugary treats, salty snack foods and hot peppery sauces.

Foods such as pizza, spaghetti, Mexican food, spicy meats such as salami, ham or pepperoni, sweet treats and chocolate are all dangerous foods to dogs. Chocolate, in fact, along

If house-training becomes very difficult or if your house-trained dog regresses to having accidents indoors, a trip to the vet should be your first course of action to ensure that a health problem is not the underlying cause.

with grapes, raisins, nuts and onions, is actually toxic to dogs. Feeding your dog the same food you eat is not recommended, because, aside from being the cause of stomach upsets or worse, it usually lacks the correct nutrients for your dog.

Ask your veterinarian for a proper brand and amount of commercial dog food for your particular dog. Ask also about additives such as an occasional scrambled egg, cooked chicken or ground meat and cooked vegetables. Adding enhancers to regular dog food should be done only occasionally and in very small amounts, and is not intended to supplement the dog's diet. Commercial dog foods are carefully formulated to meet canine nutritional requirements determined by scientific studies.

RESENTMENT

Resentment can sometimes occur when a dog feels neglected by his formerly attentive owners. Cases of a new baby or a second pet as previously described are examples of this. That's why it's so important to integrate the newcomer, whether human or animal, into the home gradually and carefully. Making sure that the dog never feels left out or neglected will help the dog accept the addition and enjoy it as well.

Another case of resentment can occur when a dog develops a

Family members' giving in to the pleading eyes of a beggar and tossing him "people food" treats can certainly result in stomach upset, possibly diarrhea and even more serious problems.

dislike for a particular person. A child who has treated the dog cruelly or an adult who has over-disciplined the dog may elicit signs of resentment in the dog. Even a visitor who has mistreated the dog in some way will not be forgotten by the dog. Every time that person comes to your home, the dog may resent his presence. The dog may shy away from the person, growl or run and hide, urinate out of fear or cling to your side for protection from future abuse.

Do not allow people to abuse your dog. They may play too roughly or scare the dog in a way that will leave a permanent impression of fear in the dog. If

Is your pup developing nuisance behaviors just to make you notice him? If that's the case, look at your own role in the problem.

you have guests coming to your home whom you suspect will intimidate your dog, unpleasant incidents can be prevented by putting the dog in another room or in his crate while such people are there.

SUBMISSIVE URINATION

This behavior is quite common in puppies and usually subsides as the puppy matures. In addition, some breeds are more prone to submissive urination than others. The secret to helping the puppy outgrow this behavior is not to recognize it at all.

Let's say you are greeting your dog upon returning from work. As you bend down to pet the dog, you notice a small puddle spreading underneath the puppy. Your first reaction is to yell "No!" and begin scolding the dog for wetting indoors. As long as you notice the accident, the dog will

Be careful how you pet and handle a submissive pup, as you do not want your cuddle to result in a puddle!

probably continue to have more of them.

Instead of yelling and making a big fuss, try the following routine. When you come home, do not greet the dog excitedly. Instead, be casual and say, "Let's go out" as you head for the door with the pup's collar and leash in your hand. Hook up the dog quickly and proceed directly to his exercise area. Once he urinates and you're sure that he's done, you can greet him outdoors. By the time you get back in the house, the excitement of the reunion will be over and the dog will be his normal self again.

In the case of a dog, puppy or adult, that urinates submissively whenever you pet him, again don't recognize the accident. Once

looking into your face. When he does, take your hand and pet him under the chin and along the sides of his face. Petting a submissive dog on the top of his head or around his face often makes the dog urinate submissively. By keeping your hands under the chin and along the sides of the head and shoulders, the dog does not react submissively.

A house-trained, well-mannered and socialized dog will adapt to new situations and be welcomed wherever you take him.

TRAVEL TROUBLES

Traveling with your dog can be fun and trouble-free if you've taught your dog the rules of the road. Having a dog that eliminates properly in a variety of places under a variety of circumstances makes traveling with Charlie a fun experience. Most show dogs are trained to relieve themselves on command. Thus training for traveling should start long before you actually begin your trip.

When you take your dog out to exercise and relieve himself, get

Any type of training becomes more challenging when you are among the distractions of a new environment that the dog can't wait to explore.

the dog wets the floor, take him out of the room, clean up the spot and say nothing about it to him when you bring him back into the room. If he gets no attention for causing an accident, he will probably realize that he can get your attention in other ways. The secret is not letting him see you clean up the accident. In other words, you don't see it, recognize it or give him attention for creating it.

In addition, instead of bending down to pet the dog, teach him to come up to your hand by raising his head and

in the habit of saying "Let's go out," "Go make" or "Potty time" (or whatever other phrase you want to use as a relief command). The dog will soon associate relieving himself with that command. Once he does, take him to other places at exercise time. At first, don't move too far away from his usual relief area. Use your usual relief command and when your dog responds by urinating or defecating, praise him lavishly.

Remember that the dog is accustomed to relieving himself in one area of your home territory. That area is usually a grassy spot filled with the familiar scents of previous droppings. Each time he returns to the area, he's stimulated to relieve himself again.

Taking the dog on a trip with you can create a whole new set of problems for the dog. For example, he will surely be expected to relieve himself on cement or stone areas, which are totally new to him. It's like moving a country dog into the city and expecting him to accept the city street as his toilet area. In addition, you won't be able to condition the dog to the new and different relief surfaces. As a result, he'll probably hold his urine and feces rather than have an "accident" on unfamiliar ground. This will ultimately result in the dog's having real accidents in motel and hotel rooms or the homes of family and friends whom you're visiting.

Labrador Retrievers are friendly dogs that like to go for rides in cars and try new things with their owners.

For a Beagle, a few sniffs of the grass are like reading a doggie tabloid...it tells him who's been here, when, with whom and what's going on.

During the training process prior to your trip, be patient with the dog until he figures out what you want from him. It may take several weeks to get him accustomed to relieving himself in different places and situations, but he will eventually learn. The praise he gets when he complies will make the lesson easier and more pleasant. Finally, always take a plastic bag with you to clean up after your dog.

PREVIOUS ACCIDENT AREAS
Dogs have olfactory senses thousands of times greater than those of humans. For example, when you think you've done a good job cleaning up an accident, your dog will continue to smell urine or feces long after the cleanup process.

The scent of urine and feces stimulates the dog to relieve himself, which is why dogs will use the same relief area over and over. Thus, to prevent an accident from recurring, the cleanup must include the removal of the scents associated with it.

Male dogs in particular are prone to urinating and defecating in areas that carry the scent of previous eliminations from either themselves or other dogs. It is their way of marking a territory. Some females are frequent markers also and will maintain the habit throughout their lives.

Hard surfaces such as tile and hardwood floors are easily cleaned and deodorized by soaking up the urine or picking up the feces with paper towels. Use a soapy solution of warm water and a cleanser to wipe the area

"IT'S IN THERE!"

If you use ammonia to clean a urine accident, the dog will most likely use that same spot again. That's because there is ammonia in urine. Hence the dog will smell the cleaning ammonia at a later time and urinate on the spot again to remark his/her territory.

clean. Rinse and let dry. When the area is dry, apply any one of several commercial products designed to deodorize pet-accident areas. Some can be purchased in spray form, which makes the process even easier.

Cleaning up a carpeted area is basically the same except that it will be necessary to blot up the urine with paper towels before scrubbing. Simply place several layers of paper towels over the spot and press down (or even stand on them). This will force the urine up into the towels. Repeat with fresh towels until the area is almost dry. Next, use the soapy warm water as before. Rinse well and towel dry

again. Wait until the area is completely dry before applying a deodorizer. For repeat offenses, you may have to have the carpet shampooed thoroughly and use a wet vacuum to clean the carpet really well.

In the case of feces on carpet, remove the stool, then scrub the area thoroughly with warm soapy water. Use paper towels to soak up the scrubbing water. Rinse well and towel dry. When the area is completely dry, apply a deodorizer.

One of the best deodorizers I know of is a solution made of equal parts water and white vinegar, because vinegar neutralizes the ammonia in urine. In the case of carpeting, I always test the solution on a hidden spot of the carpet to make sure the vinegar won't bleach out or leave a mark on the carpeting. If you choose to use a commercial product, you'll find a good selection at any well-stocked pet-supply store. If you're not sure which product to purchase, the store employees will gladly make appropriate suggestions. The cleaners based on natural ingredients often prove the most effective.

If you keep your home free of elimination odors and offer the dog a consistent relief area outdoors, and frequent opportunities to use it, it won't take long at all to have a house-trained companion. Again, patience, praise and proper management will be the keys to your success.

THE WRONG MESSAGE

I picked up my phone, and a young-sounding female voice said, "Is this Charlotte?"

"Yes," I replied.

"This is Mary. Mad Mary. Not angry Mary. This is losing-my-mind Mary and I need your help," she said in a pleading tone.

"How can I help you?" I responded.

"I have the most wonderful five-month-old Shih Tzu puppy you could ever have. And I'm going to have to give her away. I just can't seem to housebreak her and it's driving me crazy. I can't take the mess in the house anymore. And my husband feels the same way. We don't want to give her up, but we can't live like this for another week."

Thus began my involvement in one more typical house-training problem that seems to plague dozens of families with new puppies. But all is not lost, and I told Mary that when we spoke.

"A few private consultations and you and the pup will be on the same page when it comes to eliminating outdoors and keeping the house clean," I assured her.

Even though many people are attracted to toy breeds for their small size, delightful personalities and appealing looks, they often can be difficult to housebreak.

"Can you meet with me tomorrow morning?"

The next day, Mary and her husband Stan brought Freckles to meet with me. As Mary claimed, Freckles was a delightful bundle of wiggly love and happiness. She was alert, attentive, eager to please and just plain full of herself (as a Shiz Tzu should be).

The program I outlined for the three of them began that day. It has worked well for hundreds of dog owners with the same problem. It's easy to implement and quick to gain positive results. It begins with a bit of understanding why the dog does what he does and how to communicate to the dog what you want from him.

First, Mary told me that she and Stan spend hours walking the dog around the neighborhood. Up and down side streets, through open fields, in grassy areas along the side of busy roads. Freckles loves the walks and spends her entire time sniffing everything she can and looking around at exciting things such as butterflies launching and landing, leaves on the wing, newspapers tumbling across the road, an occasional rabbit bounding across their path. Each walk is an adventure for Freckles and she comes home exhausted and content with the day's excursion.

There's only one problem. Not once during the half-hour walk did Freckles stop to urinate or defecate. She was just too busy to think of elimination during the walk. However, once at home, Freckles ran off to the dining room, where she urinated. Then, moments later, she wandered into the living room and defecated there. Shortly after that, she returned to the family room, where she curled up in her soft bed and fell asleep.

When Mary found the accidents, she cleaned up the messes and scolded Freckles as she wondered why the house-training wasn't working. Was she supposed to stay outdoors with the dog for as long as it took for Freckles to void? Was she supposed to forget outdoor training and switch to newspapers in the house, which both she and Stan did not want to do? Should she try spanking Freckles every time she had an accident? Should she ignore the accidents and just hope that maturity would resolve the problem? How long could she live with a dirty house that frequently smelled of feces and/or ammonia?

In desperation, Mary called her veterinarian, who recommended that she call "this very good local trainer" (a.k.a., yours truly). So began the new training program. Freckles, it seems, was getting the wrong message from Mary and Stan. To Freckles, those long walks outdoors every day were adventures in exploration. And every day was different, so the pup never tired of the walks. After all, what canine doesn't love new and exciting things to see and smell? And who has time to think about bathroom necessities in the middle of an adventure!?

Here's the plan I prescribed. First, Freckles would be crate-trained and, when not in her crate, she would be in the same room with Mary or Stan at all times. She would no longer be given freedom to wander around the house to urinate or defecate. In addition, Freckles would wear a houseline at all times when she was out of her crate. Only when she was crated would she not wear a collar and either her houseline indoors or her regular leash outdoors.

A houseline is a long thin cord that the owner attaches to the dog's collar. Its purpose is two-fold. It acts as a security blanket for the dog. When she's wearing it, she feels attached to her pack (her owners) and thus she feels safe. For the owners, it gives them the ability to control the dog at all times. For example, if they want the dog to do something, such as come to them, all they have to do is call the dog with a happy tone of voice and give a slight tug on the end of the houseline, which the dog drags around behind her. Even though the dog is in the same room with the owners, the houseline becomes an extension of the connection between the dog and her pack leaders.

To make a houseline, buy a 6-foot length of nylon cord, similar to the kind used in Venetian blinds. Purchase a small clasp, similar to the kind found on any leash. Attach the clasp to one end of the line, but do not make a loop at the other end. Leave that end plain so it will not get caught on furniture or doorways. Instead, the line will slide easily behind the dog as she moves around a room. Most importantly, never leave the dog alone while she's wearing her houseline. If the dog must be left alone, use the crate. Period.

Abide by the author's rules of crate-training. Be sure the dog has been taught to love her crate and she enjoys being in it. If she doesn't like being there, chances are you haven't emphasized positive-training methods. However, if that's the case, don't despair. Simply go back to the beginning and repeat the training schedule. You can even give her a

Like Freckles, all house-trained Shih Tzu know the value of their crates.

Reward your pup with praise and a treat as soon as he relieves himself so he connects the voiding action with something positive, and thus gets the idea of why he's there.

small biscuit to entice and reward her to get into her crate during the retraining process.

For a problem dog, be sure to set up and adhere to a workable exercise schedule based on the age of the dog. No matter what age the dog, you must arrange to get the dog outdoors as frequently as needed. The big thing about taking Freckles outdoors is the way you do it, not how long you stay. First, decide in advance which area you want the dog to use as a relief area. As you've learned, walking all over the neighborhood proves counter-productive to the house-training lessons. Just as humans have bathrooms and restrooms, so must Freckles have a special area which she associates with elimination. It's not a play area, an exploration area or a visit-with-the-neighbors area. It's for doing her business and nothing more.

With her collar and leash on, walk her to her relief area every time you take her out of her crate.

Stand there for five minutes—no more—and ignore her while she sniffs around and investigates the spot. Incidentally, her area should be no larger than about 10 feet by 15 feet. Don't give her the whole back yard! You'll just begin the confusion all over again.

If she voids during the five-minute stay, reward her with a biscuit, praise lavishly and bring her back into the house immediately. Once inside, she should be hooked up to her houseline and given freedom to play in the same room with you. If she doesn't void during the time outdoors, bring her back into the house and put her back into her crate.

Wait a half-hour and then hook her up to her leash again and take her back to her outdoor relief area. Once more, stand there and let her sniff around, but don't talk to her. Sooner or later, she'll have to void and at that time you'll reward and praise excitedly. Then bring her into the house, put on the houseline and give her room freedom again.

Depending on her age, you should know by past experience about how long she can wait before she'll need to go out again. Keep her with you at all times. Be sure she comes with you as you move from room to room. Watch her closely and anticipate her needs anytime you see her circling, sniffing or acting as if she's about to either urinate or defecate. At that point, get her outdoors to her area quickly and repeat the five-minute silent wait routine. By not talking to her when she's in her area, you allow her to concentrate on the smells of the place plus the purpose for her being there. When you talk to her, she doesn't focus on her reason for being there.

Soon she'll begin to anticipate going to her area, and she may even begin to let you know by some particular behavior that she wants to go out. A little whine, a short bark, pacing back and forth to a doorway and coming to you as if she were trying to tell you something are all signs that dogs give to express their relief needs. As the dog matures, she'll develop signals of her own design. Watch and learn from them.

While you're retraining Freckles, you will no longer take those long and lengthy walks around town. Only when she's completely house-trained should you teach her that the outdoors is a place for fun and play as well as for elimination. Don't confuse the dog while she's learning. Save the

SIX MONTHS OF PATIENCE

Most dogs can be house-trained in 7 to 14 days. Keep in mind, however, that puppies do not have full muscle control of their excretory functions until they're six months of age; thus, frequent opportunities to eliminate are a necessity until they mature.

outdoors for voiding only. Do your playing indoors until she's clean and reliable. And never play in her relief area, whether during the training process or after she's house-trained. It's her bathroom!

The end of Freckles's story is a happy one. Mary and Stan followed the house-training routine that I prescribed. Within three days of using her new area, Freckles urinated in the grass and Stan really celebrated with her. Later that same day, she defecated outdoors. She also clearly demonstrated that she had made the connection between a biscuit treat and praise with doing her business in her own area. Three weeks later, Mary and Stan considered her training remarkable and they're thrilled that Freckles will be with them forever.

She still wears her houseline and seems to really enjoy it. She's very sure of herself when it's on. Now Stan will begin to reduce its length by a foot a week until the houseline is a mere 6 inches long. Depending on her eventual reaction to the short piece of cord hanging from her collar, she may wear it forever or she may be willing to give it up as unnecessary. That will depend on Freckles herself, and Stan and Mary will know what she wants by her actions. When the time comes, Freckles will let it go. She'll be self-confident and secure, no longer getting the wrong message from her pack members.

RELIEVING VS. MARKING

WHAT'S THE DIFFERENCE?

A dog relieves himself when the dog's brain tells him it's time to empty his bladder. It is strictly a functional event designed by nature to rid the body of waste fluid and any impurities in the kidneys. This behavior is a necessary bodily function in both males and females. Dogs and other animals and could not survive without this normal behavior.

Marking is primarily used by male dogs as a method of communication. Dogs use marking behaviors to signal to other dogs that they have been in a particular area and are claiming that territory as their domain. Marking is executed with precision and often repeated many times in a single area. For example, a male may lift his leg and mark a spot on a tree trunk. Then he'll mark again on a nearby telephone pole and once again on a spot of grass a few feet away from the tree. A female will squat and sometimes lift one leg off the ground as she deposits a small amount of urine on a spot. Occasionally a dominant female dog will develop marking behaviors as well.

Markings consist of only a few drops of urine, never large amounts. In this way, the dog puts down only enough urine to serve as identification, thus reserving enough urine to mark other

Outdoors is the only place for a dog the size of the St. Bernard to relieve himself.

places. In contrast, when a dog urinates to relieve his bladder, he finds a suitable place and empties his bladder completely. Consequently, marking spots are often difficult to see whereas relief spots consist of easily seen puddles.

When these two behaviors happen in the home, it can spell trouble in many ways: trouble for the dog; trouble for the owner and trouble for the house itself. If a dog has an accident and relieves himself indoors, the resulting puddle is usually found right away. Cleanup follows quickly after that.

On the other hand, marking indoors can be a real problem. Because the markings are made up of such tiny amounts of urine, finding them is frequently impossible. If the culprit is a small or toy breed, the dog may mark indoors for years before his habit is discovered.

BEDROOM/KITCHEN VS. BATHROOM

As a rule, dogs won't eliminate near their bed or food. Therefore when house-training a dog to indoors, be sure the elimination area is not near the dog's bed or eating area. Actually, it's best to train the dog to paper in a room other than the one where he eats and sleeps. Making that clear distinction will help him learn quickly.

Male dogs sometimes retain the squatting behavior when urinating for relief.

I know of a case that was probably several years old before the owners discovered the situation. And it wasn't until the people began smelling a strange odor in the house that they found the problem. "At first we couldn't figure out what that smell was," reported the lady. "Then one day my husband mentioned that the odor reminded him of urine. But my Yorkie, Tiger, is housebroken, so we never suspected him of being the culprit! A few days later, I discovered that the corner of our bedspread had turned a dark yellow. I felt the carpet beneath and found it damp. I took a paper towel and soaked up the damp spot and that's when we discovered the urine.

"Further investigation around the house turned up a number of Tiger's favorite spots, such as the corner of the sofa, one of the doorways in the hall, an ottoman

Your macho mastiff, even if he is neutered, is more likely to develop marking behaviors than a more submissive dog.

in the family room. We're amazed that he's been doing this for so long and yet we never realized it until the house began to smell," she said.

This is very typical of toy dogs that mark indiscriminately indoors and out. Males that are not neutered, called intact males, often exhibit this behavior. Natural instincts create their need for territorial marking to notify other males to stay away. Large dogs that mark indoors are usually discovered early on because the amount of urine deposited on furniture and doorways is usually large enough to be easily identified. And if there is an unspayed female in the neighborhood, they mark even more regularly.

Punishing the dog for marking is often not successful, because his hormones rather than learned rules of conduct dictate his behavior. Thus

neutering a male dog at an early age, usually before his body begins to produce testosterone, serves to limit marking behavior to areas outdoors where the scent of other males is present. Even this behavior can be controlled by training so the dog does not mark undesirable places.

Dominant dogs are a lot more likely to mark than submissive ones. Thus it behooves the owner to observe his puppy as he develops into maturity to determine where the dog fits in the pack order of the home. For example, a training class for puppies under 20 weeks of age or a basic obedience class for dogs over 5 months of age can do wonders for dog and owner in this regard.

First, the owner will learn which type of personality his puppy possesses. The owner will be taught how to train the dog in self-control and to teach him how, when and where to relieve himself. The owner also will learn how to teach the dog not to mark in unacceptable places. Finally, he'll learn about neutering and spaying and why this procedure helps create an ideal canine companion.

In the case of Tiger, the little Yorkie, and other dogs like him, neutering at an older age, long after a male has established a habit of marking indoors and out, may or may not help curb his marking. In some dogs, reduction of testosterone production will cause the dog to lose a desire for territorial marking whereas in other dogs the habit itself is so ingrained that they continue urine-marking. That's why it is so important to neuter and spay dogs when they are young, before their hormones cause undesirable behaviors to emerge.

THE "ON-THE-GO" DOG

Many dog owners get their pets with the idea of making the dogs active companions in their busy lifestyles. For example, some people take their dogs shopping with them. Others frequent restaurants that offer outdoor dining areas so their dogs can accompany them.

Not long ago, a friend and I visited St. Petersburg, Florida. My friend brought along her sweet little Toy Poodle, Molly. We ate lunch at a restaurant that caters to people and their dogs. Molly sat in a chair at the table

Poodles of all sizes are known as very bright and easy-to-train dogs, so it's no wonder why they are such well-loved companions.

and never once did anything to annoy or embarrass us. We gave her a few dog biscuits to eat and the waitress brought her a small bowl of water.

Molly settled nicely in the chair while we enjoyed a leisurely lunch and conversation. All the while, a steady stream of other customers walked by our table and stopped to admire our well-behaved canine companion. When we left, the waitress remarked that serving us was indeed a pleasure. Needless to say, we left feeling very proud of Miss Molly!

ELIMINATE THE NEGATIVE

Most well-trained working dogs—guard dogs, police K-9 dogs, guide and hearing ear dogs—are trained to eliminate on command. Teaching the dog to control his elimination times and places helps him focus on whatever you want the dog to do with you.

As we left the restaurant, Molly trotted along beside us yet never stopped to sniff or squat to mark the area. However, I have seen her occasionally mark a spot. Why then didn't she mark in or around the restaurant, since it was a new place to her?

Answer: Molly was taught selective marking. In other words, my friend taught Molly that there is a time and a place for marking and she would signal the dog when the appropriate times occur. Molly has honored that rule ever since she was house-trained as a youngster.

Another friend has a lovely Golden Retriever named Johnson. That big boy travels with his owner to work, to go shopping, to go fishing, to go boating and to advanced obedience classes, and he never marks inappropriately. Like Molly, Johnson has been taught when and where marking is permissible. The dog never lifts his leg in public places or in new places unless he's given the signal to do so.

Both dogs are frequently taken to the homes of their owners' friends, yet they never exhibit marking behavior even though those places are not familiar to the dogs. There is probably nothing more embarrassing than taking your dog to a friend's home and having the dog lift his leg on the friend's furniture. You can be sure, if that happens, your dog will never be welcome at that person's home again!

Despite the fact that marking is instinctual behavior, dogs can be taught self-control with regard to marking. It isn't difficult to teach a dog not to mark unless he's given the OK signal. Training for controlled marking and general urination for both sexes begins with clearly identifying a specific relief area to the dog. If he attempts to urinate or defecate in an inappropriate area, give a short, light pop on the lead to get his attention. Simultaneously say "No" and immediately take him to an area which you feel is appropriate. As soon as he begins to sniff the suitable area, tell him "Good boy. Go hurry up" (or whatever relief command you normally use).

Once the dog learns to urinate and/or mark in his own relief area, you can broaden the behavior by giving the dog additional areas to use. Introduce the dog to one new area at a time and be sure to use his normal, familiar relief command each time you take him out. Eventually the dog will respond to your relief command wherever he is. Thus, when you go to visit someone or you take him out in public, he will restrain himself until he is guided to a specific area where you give his relief command.

When you think about it, you never see service dogs mark or urinate in inappropriate places. Guide dogs for the blind, assistance dogs that help disabled persons, police K-9 dogs—all lead busy lives. They travel to many places, yet they never break the rules of urination or territorial marking. Interestingly, many K-9 dogs are intact males yet with correct training they learn self-control. Pet dogs can be trained to display those same good manners, too. All it takes is a little know-how, some patience, determination, praise and a desire to have a clean dog of whom you can be proud.

A guide dog in training. Most service dogs are taught to eliminate on command so that their relief times do not interfere with their work.

A true Golden-oldie! Humans and dogs share one of the most noticeable characteristics of old age—gray hair.

THE SENIOR DOG

The success you achieve with your puppy's house-training hopefully will extend through your dog's adult years, though problems can begin once your adult enters his senior years. Seniors can become unhouse-broken due to the confusion that can come with old age, sometimes called cognitive dysfunction, as well as health problems and various other factors.

HOW OLD IS OLD?

Different breeds of dog age at different rates. Mixed breeds usually age at rates unique to that particular dog simply because the genetic makeup is individual to each dog. For example, one dog of Labrador Retriever/Cocker Spaniel heritage might show signs of aging at six years of age while a litter-mate might not show any signs of aging until he is ten years old.

Generally speaking, small-breed dogs have longer lifespans than those of large- and giant-breed dogs. A university veterinary medical school did a research program on aging in dogs. They examined a wide variety of toy dogs, small dogs, medium dogs, large dogs and giant breeds. The results of that study showed Great Danes, for example, as being old at the age of six years. Some toy breeds live 16 to 17 years. The average medium-sized dog is generally considered old between 10 and 13 years of age. Because each breed is unique and the overall health of the individual dog contributes to the dog's longevity, owners should consult with breeders and veterinarians for expected lifespans and senior status. For healthcare

Maltese, like many small dogs, have long life expectancies, usually well into the double digits.

There are hundreds of stories of dogs injured in accidents that should have died, but some invisible and unexplained source of strength takes control of them and they defy death. Others, on the other hand, seem to have an inborn trait of defeatism. They cry and whimper over minor discomforts and problems. They take an all-out negative attitude toward fighting back and surviving. No amount of training or human interaction and support seems to help them develop inner strength. They seem predestined to submit to life's difficulties, no matter the degree of intensity. In these cases, there is little anyone can do to change the course of events leading to the end of life. Fortunately, these negative-type dogs are few and far between.

Most dogs that live normal,

The vet may suggest that you go back to a three-meal-a-day plan with your senior. You also will incorporate extra relief trips each day, also on a consistent schedule.

purposes, most veterinarians consider dogs seniors at seven or eight years of age.

One additional aspect of aging is common to most mammals, including dogs. That is mental attitude. It's often referred to as "the will to live." Just as with humans, the will to live is frequently responsible for a being's survival despite unbelievable odds against it such as with cancer or other long-term illnesses in people.

SENIOR RESTROOM RULES

As your dog becomes a senior, you likely will have to limit the amount of time he spends in his crate. Although he may sleep more and more, he also gets a little creaky and has trouble getting up and around. Arthritis makes the crate less and less comfortable for a senior dog. You will have to keep a close eye on him, encourage him to go out often, give him plenty of time while he's outside and be ready to wake up in the middle of the night to let him outside.

Some feel that mixed breeds are hardier, longer-lived dogs, as they are not prone to the genetic problems seen in some pure-breds, while others feel that this theory of "hybrid vigor" in mixed breeds is a myth.

Hopefully, you've been taking care of your dog's teeth for his whole life. A healthy mouth gives the senior dog an advantage for overall good health.

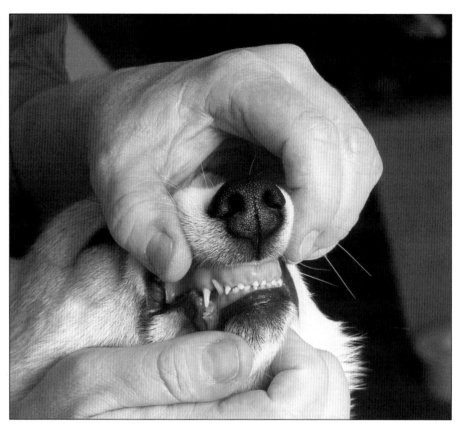

healthy lifestyles with caring owners have naturally healthy attitudes and age gracefully without too many problems. In addition, the process is made even more comfortable when owners are aware of the numerous signs of aging.

SIGNS OF AGING
Following are many of the changes that appear in dogs as they age. Not all dogs experience every one of the changes, but you will certainly be able to identify enough to recognize the onset of the senior years:

- The dog's muzzle turns gray;
- The tone of his bark changes from loud and crisp to softer and muted;
- Coat becomes drier and thinner.
- Bumps or open skin sores;
- Eyes change color;
- Noticeable sight loss or pupils do not constrict in bright light;
- Diminished stamina; tires more easily;

- Movement is slower and often obviously painful;
- Change in normal urination or bowel movement habits;
- Wets bed during sleep.
- Hearing difficulty—not as acute or appears not to hear specific types of sounds;
- Sleeps more than usual, sleeps more deeply, slower to awaken;
- Excessive panting, coughing and/or drooling;
- Bad breath, red or swollen gums, loose teeth, bleeding gums;
- Changes in appetite or eating habits;
- Drinks more or less water than normal;
- Less active than in previous years;
- Unexplainable weight gain or loss;
- Vomiting.

HEALTH CONDITIONS IN THE OLDER DOG

Since no one organ of the body is a separate entity that does not affect other body parts, owners must be aware of their senior dogs' health and condition whenever assessing house-training issues or attempting to retrain the dog. For example, periodontal disease, a painful inflammatory condition of the gums, sends damaging bacteria to the kidneys which, in turn, can create kidney infections. Those infections can be responsible for urinary accidents in the home.

Other vital organs such as the heart, lungs and liver are also affected by teeth and gum problems. Actually, dogs over the age of seven years can develop a variety of health problems, which often result in poor bladder and bowel control. Even the long-term use of certain medications can result in kidney abnormalities. Consequently, having a senior dog requires certain considerations from the owner that do not apply to puppies and younger dogs.

Your senior dog is still the same loving companion that just wants to be near those he loves. Make his golden years happy ones!

MANAGING THE ELIMINATION NEEDS OF OLDER DOGS

As the dog ages, the owner needs to increase his awareness of the dog's more frequent need to relieve himself. In addition, the owner must take note of the dog's changing elimination behavior habits. For example, for the first eight years of her life, my own Toy Poodle, Ginger, had two bowel movements a day. Her elimination habits were so well established that I could predict exactly when she would urinate and when she would defecate. However, as she began to age her elimination habits changed.

She sometimes had bowel movements once a day, sometimes three times a day and occasionally twice a day. I no longer could predict her elimination habits. Now, at age 17 years, she eats small meals three times a day because her digestive system can't cope with larger quantities of food at a single feeding. Consequently, she has more frequent bowel movements, just as she did when she was a tiny puppy eating three meals a day.

As the dog's habits change, so do the dog's signals to go out. Ginger used to come and sit in front of me to let me know she wanted out. Now she wanders

Be sure to provide soft bedding for your senior, as he will appreciate the cushioning for his achy bones.

Many dogs remain active in their senior years and will enjoy the same activities with their owners, even if at a slower pace.

aimlessly around the room, often panting, and acting restless as if she can't make up her mind about what she wants. In fact, her elimination habits have now become a guessing game for me, and I am constantly alert to her more frequent needs.

Just as she did when she was a tiny puppy, Ginger frequently wakes me in the middle of the night to go out. She sleeps in her crate beside my bed, and I'm awakened by her heavy panting and soft whimpers. I simply take her out, she does what she needs to do and we immediately go back to bed until morning.

More medical attention may be needed to maintain quality and length of life for the older dog as well. In addition, your veterinarian may recommend a particular brand

of dog food for older dogs and/or a dietary supplement to be added to his regular food. These diet changes can help the senior control his elimination needs, too.

I often think how similar to humans dogs are. We start life depending on others for our total care. Then mid-life finds us independent and capable of caring for ourselves. Finally, old age sets in and we're back to the need for total care once again, which we aptly term the "Depends" stage. The cycle of life is much the same for dogs as it is for humans. Senior dogs especially need us as much now as they did at the beginning of life. The senior dog has given his family many years of unconditional love and devotion, and now it's the family's turn to be there for the dog.

FREQUENTLY ASKED QUESTIONS AND ANSWERS

My puppy urinates on the floor every time someone bends over to pet her. How can I stop her from doing this?

This behavior is called submissive urination. It is caused by an involuntary relaxation of the bladder muscles, not the dog's need to void. It often occurs in puppies, particularly females, and sometimes in adult dogs. The accident is usually not a large puddle, such as when the dog urinates to empty her bladder.

"How can I make my owners happy?" is the question most frequently asked by pups. Dogs want to please us and we just need to show them how.

Rather it is only a few drops of urine or a small spot instead of a puddle.

This behavior occurs frequently in submissive puppies and adults. It is nature's way of telling other dogs when they meet that the individual is not a dominant threat. If you have the opportunity to observe two strange dogs meeting and investigating each other, you may observe this behavior. The submissive dog will also pull back her ears, drop her tail and generally assume a submissive posture.

By establishing who is submissive and who is dominant, nature assures a peaceful encounter and the ultimate preservation of the species. If, for example, all dogs were dominant, there would be nothing but chaos and constant fighting for dominance.

Unfortunately, many owners reprimand the dog when this submissive urination occurs. In the dog's mind, therefore, the behavior elicits the owner's attention and thus creates a desire for more attention. The dog thinks "When I pee, I get lots of attention, so I'll do it again." Unfortunately, this is exactly the opposite behavior that you're trying to elicit from the dog.

Before you begin a program to correct this situation, have your veterinarian examine your dog to be sure there is no physical reason for her having these accidents. Be sure to tell your vet exactly when and where these mistakes occur.

The solution, then, is to downplay the accident, get the dog away from the area and get her focused on something pleasant. When the dog is out of the area of the accident, soak up the urine with paper towels and then wash the floor with a mixture of a small amount of vinegar and soapy water. Towel-dry as thoroughly as possible. There are, incidentally, commer-cial products that can be used to clean up accidents and render them odorless. Most are available in pet-supply stores.

To prevent this from happening again, develop a habit of not greeting the dog in any way. When you or another person enters a room, casually say something like "Hello, Trixie. Let's go out." Then quickly go to the door and call the dog to follow you. Attach the collar and lead and get the dog out to her voiding area immediately.

Once the dog urinates in her exercise area, you can bend down and greet the dog just as you would have done previously at the front door. It may take you several weeks of using this routine of initially ignoring the dog at greeting time, but eventually the dog will learn to control her bladder and stay dry when you or another person enters the home.

You will be so proud of your clean dog!

The cardinal rule for correcting submissive wetting is never to recognize the accident and praise lavishly for urinating outdoors. Any recognition, such as the dog's watching you clean up an accident or your yelling at the dog for having an accident indoors, will assure you of more accidents, not fewer. Never let the dog see you clean up a spot in the house and do make a big fuss over your wonderful clean dog that urinates outdoors.

Both my husband and I have unpredictable work schedules so we never know when we'll be able to get the dog outside to eliminate. What can we do to ensure that the dog won't have accidents in the house?

There are two answers to this question, and the one that applies to you will depend upon what size of dog you have. If, for example, you have a small- to medium-sized dog, you can train the dog to use newspaper, preferably placed in a laundry room or bathroom. That way, the dog can void whenever he feels the need without having an accident in other areas of the home. I know of a number of dogs that eliminate outdoors in the evenings and on weekends when their owners are home to take them out. During the day, however, those same dogs use newspaper indoors and never have accidents on carpeting or in other areas of the home.

In most of those cases, the owner began by training the puppy to paper upon his arrival in the home. Then, as the pup began to grow up, the owner would take the dog outside whenever possible. Lots of praise followed each elimination until the dog learned that going outdoors was OK, too.

Finally, the owner kept the paper down and the dog automatically gravitated to it when the owner was away at work. As the pup became an adult dog, the owner did not change the arrangement and the dog adjusted to his dual elimination habit comfortably.

Now let's address the large-breed dog and his needs. Paper-training a large dog is just not practical. Big dogs mean big puddles and piles, making indoor cleanup rather unpleasant, not to mention rather odoriferous.

The second alternative to the unpredictable schedule problem is to hire someone to come into your home and take the dog for a walk around noon of each workday. In the case of a puppy under six months of age, the dog walker should come in twice a day, once in the middle of the morning and again at mid-afternoon.

As the dog matures into an adult, he can hold his urine and stool for longer periods of time.

An adult dog seems to adapt to his owner's work schedule and, probably because most of the day is spent snoozing, he just doesn't need to go out very often. Each owner's schedule and each dog is unique. Therefore there is no way to predict the timetable your dog will or will not develop as he matures.

No matter how often I take my dog out, he urinates in his crate almost every day. How can I stop this?

First of all, if your dog is a puppy, crate accidents are usually just that. Accidents. Possibly you're not taking the dog out often enough, particularly if he's still young. Puppies need to go often because their bladder muscles are not fully developed until they are at least six months of age. A puppy, then, should be taken outdoors every one to two hours. Alternatively, you may be offering the puppy water too late at night, so he can't hold it until morning. Maybe you're keeping the puppy crated too often or for too long a period at any one time. Either way, the dog is being forced to relieve himself in his crate because he can't hold his urine long enough for you to take him out.

If your dog is an adult that has an occasional accident in his

A dog does not want to soil his crate, but he can only "hold it" for so long.

A large dog means a large mess if you don't take his training to heart!

The crate is such an important tool in your house-training success. You must make a positive connection; the more the dog loves his den, the harder he will try to keep it clean.

give him lots of praise for being such a good dog.

Is the dog over seven years of age? As the dog enters his senior years, his bladder function slows down and he may naturally need to urinate more frequently.

When the dog has an accident in his crate, how do you react? Do you yell at the dog, punish the dog, reprimand the dog in any way? Do you take the dog out and for the next few minutes go on and on about "Bad boy. You wet in your crate. You're such a bad dog!"

All of this attention simply serves to teach the dog that wetting in his crate will get lots of attention from you. Oh, he doesn't like it when you holler at him, but getting you to notice him is better than not being noticed at all. Thus he'll continue to have more accidents to make you notice him.

What you need to do is get the dog outdoors to his relief area more often. If he goes, praise lavishly and tell him how wonderful he is to "Go out." Do not mention his accident or his crate. When you return to the house, keep the dog away from his crate area until you clean up the accident, remove his soiled blanket and put down fresh bedding. Be sure to use some vinegar and soapy water for cleaning to remove any scent of urine in the crate.

crate, ask yourself these questions: Am I keeping the dog crated too long at any one time? When you take the dog out, does he focus on relieving himself? Or is the dog so busy looking around, sniffing everything and totally forgetting why he is outside?

That's why training the dog to a relief area helps—when the dog reaches his relief area, he automatically assumes "relief mode." A relief command such as "Go potty" keeps the dog on track. In addition, too much chatter to the dog while he's there only serves to distract him from what he's supposed to be doing. After you give him the relief command, stop talking to the dog and let him concentrate on the business at hand. Once he's voided, that's the time to

The next time you put him in his crate, say only nice, encouraging things (don't bring up his past piddly offense). Be sure to get him outdoors more frequently and, if necessary, restrict his water consumption to small drinks instead of great quantities of water at each drink.

I've found that once the habit of eliminating in the crate is established, it is almost impossible to break the dog of this habit. Many people who work with dogs professionally claim that "once a dirty dog, always a dirty dog." To prevent this from happening to your dog, you might try starting over from the beginning and retrain the dog as if he were a little puppy who requires frequent trips outdoors.

One other solution to the problem, that the author has used successfully, is feeding the dog in his crate. Since dogs naturally will not void where they eat or sleep, turning his crate into his sleeping *and* eating place may encourage him to void elsewhere rather than in the crate. Couple that with not overdoing crate time and frequent trips to his relief area and you may have your answer.

Always remember to ignore accidents and recognize positive behavior when it happens. Since most dogs are eager to please their owners, this regimen will encourage the dog to seek your attention for desired behavior rather than for undesirable accidents.

Both my husband and I work and our two teenagers get home from school before we do. I ask them to take the dog out as soon as they get home, but sometimes they forget and the dog has accidents in the house. What can I do about preventing house accidents before my husband and I get home?

Since you can't buy your dog a larger bladder or stronger muscles, let's fix the real problem. It's time to retrain your kids! Teenagers can be very irresponsible, and parents need to keep control of them. Establish that taking the dog out immediately upon their arrival home is a standing rule. No exceptions. That means exercising the dog before they have snacks, call friends, start homework, etc.

Positive attention while the dog is in the crate will make him feel part of his surroundings, not isolated.

Remember, a busy pup is a happy pup, so make sure he's occupying himself in acceptable ways.

When you have a dog and children of any age, you must train the children as well as the dog. Explain to the children that the dog has been quiet and probably sleeping most of the day while no one was home. Their coming home wakes the dog and makes him realize that he needs to eliminate. Like the children, your dog needs to have a regular schedule of activities, too. Thus he's depending on

Wire exercise pens come in different shapes, sizes and heights.

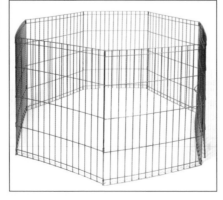

them to get him out to his potty area as soon as they get home. Since the children get home before you and your husband, the dog's needs become their responsibility.

Once the teenagers get in the habit of taking the dog out reliably, they'll do it automatically, so persevere and expect them to share the responsibility of caring for the dog. After all, it is the *family* dog. Teaching children to assume their share of chores helps them grow up to be responsible, caring adults.

I live in a home with an open floor plan (no doorways between the living room, kitchen and den) and I'm having trouble confining the puppy to house-train him. How can I control where he goes without gates or doorways to contain him?

Purchase a good-sized exercise pen (sometimes called an ex-pen). It's a pen you can easily set up in any room in minutes. It's convenient, safe, lightweight and portable. Exercise pens commonly are used by show-dog handlers and breeders when they travel to shows and even at home when they have more dogs than crates. The pens control their dogs while still allowing the dogs to move around and have more freedom than a crate offers.

Most large pet-supply stores

carry ex-pens. They are also available from the major dog-supply catalogs, either by mail order or online. You can probably find some of these catalogs at your veterinarian's office, groomer's shop, training school and dog club, or by surfing the Internet. For all their utility and durability, ex-pens are very affordable. They come in a variety of sizes ranging from 4-sided all the way up to pens made of 12 panels. Heightwise, they come in 24-, 36- and 48-inch heights. For example, an ex-pen of 12 panels in any of the three heights (depending on the dog's size) gives the dog a good amount of space in which to move around.

They are usually constructed of 9- or 11-gauge wire, making them sturdy yet easy enough to fold up and move from place to place. Since they fold flat for storing, they also travel well in most car trunks or SUVs. They're ideal for use when you go on vacation or visit friends and relatives. They help you control the dog's activities in any room of your home while you're busy with your own activities.

Ex-pens are ideal for dog owners with toddlers and small children. The dog can see everything that's going on in the house while the children remain safe from chewing puppy teeth and bounding puppy paws and sharp nails. The dog remains safe from little hands that like to pull ears and tails, poke eyes and noses—not to mention those giant puppy-hugs that can squeeze a growing pup too roughly.

In short, ex-pens are inexpensive, good for dogs, good for you and good for your home and family.

I have a seven-month-old male Norfolk Terrier. He's a wonderful dog, but sometimes he lifts his leg and urinates on me. Why does he do that and how can I stop him from doing it?

Your dog is not urinating because he needs to empty his bladder. He's marking you as part of his territory. He's saying, "You belong to me and other dogs need to stay away." If your dog is not neutered, he is

Terriers are bright, inquisitive and alert, but can be stubborn when it comes to training.

The Norfolk Terrier who relieves himself where he should outdoors...

producing hormones that in turn produce male behavioral habits such as marking. He is a true adolescent at seven months of age. If the dog has been neutered and is still marking, either he still has hormones in his system because he's only recently been neutered or he's just a dominant personality that makes him assertive regardless of hormonal production.

Either way, you're going to have to train him not to lift his leg except in approved areas. To do that, take him out to his exercise area, tell him to go and

praise lavishly when he does. Then leave the area and move to an area previously off-limits.

Watch him carefully as he begins sniffing the new spot. Just before he begins to lift his leg, say "No mark!" and give the leash a short tug toward you and away from the area of interest. When he looks at you and lifts his head up off the ground, tell him he's a good boy and move away with him.

Take him to a variety of previously unexplored places following the incident. Each time he sniffs and prepares to mark the new spot, repeat "No mark!" Be sure to praise generously when he looks at you and turns away from the area he's investigating.

Whenever he begins sniffing your feet, ankles or legs, watch him carefully. Remind him "No mark!" and immediately give a small tug on the leash and divert his attention to something different. As you begin moving around, say things like "Let's go see the bird. Where's your ball? Let's take a walk." Get him involved in thinking about something other than marking you or anything else. Once he learns to focus on acceptable activities and emptying his bladder in areas designated for the purpose, he will learn to stop marking.

Remember that positive attention for any behavior will likely be repeated, so focus on good actions and be short and stern with undesirable actions. For example, standing around and allowing the dog to sniff the area to excess will only encourage him to do more of it. Instead, take a brisk walk and keep him moving so he won't have time to sniff and get into marking mode. Playing fetch and investigating new places without marking can be positive experiences that automatically replace marking. Keeping a sharp eye on your dog when he's near you

...is a clean dog with a very happy owner!

will give you time to prevent his marking you, too. Also, watch him closely whenever he's around other people, as he may try to mark them as well.

Most importantly, you must break the marking habit as soon as you notice it developing. The longer a dog marks, the more difficult it will be to change that behavior later on. And nobody appreciates a dog that urinates inappropriately. When you think about your dog and his marking habit, take comfort in knowing that many dogs are trained to refrain from marking, like those near-perfect assistance dogs and K-9 workers, and your dog can be, too. Good timing, patience and praise will solve your problem.

Unless in a fenced yard or enclosure, your pup should always be on leash. Springer Spaniels love exploring the outdoors and his off-leash excursions could lead him into danger.

After too much time to sniff around outdoors, puppy lost all interest in relieving himself... until he got back inside, that is.

We have a five-month-old Springer Spaniel puppy named Josh. I always take him to his relief area. My husband, however, refuses to do that. Instead he wants to walk around the block with Josh. He says the dog should be able to go on long walks or jogging with him and training while he's young is better than going to the same area all the time. Who's right about this?

Your husband has an admirable idea and one that's healthy for both him and his dog. However, house-training a five-month-old puppy should not include long walks around the block. A young puppy out exploring the world is so busy sniffing and scratching that he totally forgets about his elimination needs. When the pup gets home, however, he remembers he needs to void, so he runs into a room of the house and does his business.

In all likelihood, Josh will forget that his long strolls with dad are actually "business trips." Being a sporting dog, Josh is genetically programmed to love the outdoors, and his thoughts will turn to fetching and flushing anything that moves. In other words, that's not quite what you have in mind when you begin a house-training program.

Your idea of taking Josh to his own potty area is correct for a pup his age. Be sure to keep his visits to his area frequent and short and praise generously when he voids. Your husband's goal of long walks and jogging will be realized very shortly, but he must be patient until then.

Josh should not take long walks before his little body is ready for the physical stress involved in hiking and jogging. Wait until the young dog's bones are fully developed before you expect him to perform as an adult. A Springer Spaniel, for example, will most likely realize full muscle and bone development at about one year of age. Forced exercise before this time can cause permanent bone damage, so train cautiously.

Finally, making trips to his elimination area and going for walks (or other exercise) are two separate activities. Training in the proper sequence of using his relief area first and then walking will produce a healthy and fit dog that is also completely house-trained. That's a combination for a happy, successful relationship with your canine friend for many years to come.

Whenever I yell at my dog, she rolls over on her side and wets. I keep telling her "No wet" but she just keeps doing it. Unfortunately, she wets no matter where she is (indoors or out), and this habit is ruining my carpet. How can I prevent this behavior?

Raising your voice in anger is obviously upsetting to your dog. She recognizes your tone as being unfriendly and she becomes fearful. She's probably a very submissive individual and that characteristic along with your verbal expression of annoyance trigger her defense mechanism.

Incidentally, this submissive wetting is seen more in female dogs than in males. It's also very common in puppies, so if your dog is still young, chances are she will outgrow this habit if you handle it correctly. Yelling at her will not solve the problem. She

drops down on her side, rolls over and urinates out of fear. That, in turn, makes you angry, so you yell at her. That reaction on your part makes her even more fearful. In other words, it's a vicious cycle and it will continue until you change your response to the initial behavior that started the whole thing.

There is good news regarding this problem. You can change the whole scenario by simply focusing on the original behavior that caused you to become angry. You need to find a better way of dealing with your dog than raising your voice. It's obvious that your yelling is what causes the floodgates to open in the first place. Examine the behavior of your dog to determine how would be best to handle each situation without raising your voice. Here are some more effective (quieter and drier) ways to respond to a variety of common misbehaviors.

Let's say, for example, your dog is a puppy and you catch her

The belly-up position is a classic submissive posture. A pup who shows these body-language signals may also be prone to submissive urination.

Encouraging good habits means distracting the pup away from a bad behavior and directing him to a good behavior. For example, when pup is chewing on something forbidden, tell him "No," take it away and offer him a proper chew toy.

chewing on a forbidden item, your shoe or the corner of a chair. Or maybe you catch her stealing tissues or paper towels from the trash. A common habit of puppies is to grab your pant leg and play tug-of-war with it while you're wearing the pants. Your pup probably also has discovered that barking gets lots of recognition from family members, even though most of it is unpleasant. (At least it's recognition and that's better than being ignored.)

These undesirable behaviors and other ones can be found in both adult dogs and in puppies. Changing the behavior from something you don't like to something you find acceptable is easy to do when you know how. First, let's look at the reason why the annoying habit began in the first place. Then we'll address the correction.

Puppies chew because they're teething and their gums hurt. Chewing and gnawing ease the pain in the gums. Adult dogs will sometimes chew forbidden items because they're frustrated or anxious, particularly when they find themselves alone in the house. It's called separation anxiety, and it can be corrected with the help of your veterinarian or a professional behavior consultant.

Puppies love to grab tissues, toilet paper, paper towels, socks, soft sneakers, items of clothing, etc. They will hurry off to favorite spots and proceed to chew on their stolen prizes. You respond to your pup's doing this by yelling "Stop that!" and you chase the dog around the house to retrieve the stolen item, and finally you punish the dog for misbehaving.

Most of these behaviors happen when the dog decides she wants your attention. In other words, they are her way of saying, "I want you to notice me. Give me some attention. I want someone to play with me." She even does things like playing tug-of-war with your pants and excessive barking to get your attention despite the fact that they're annoying. She has learned that being naughty is an effective method of getting attention even though she doesn't like the negative aspects of it. You, in turn, fall right into her trap and give her attention in the hopes of stopping the undesirable behavior.

The dog recognizes that her behavior gets your attention, yet your responses cause the dog to be fearful and submissive. Being submissive, in turn, often includes loss of bladder control, resulting in the dog's wetting in the house.

Before you begin a program to correct your dog's naughty habits, try to determine why they occur in the first place. Ask yourself some questions: When does the dog do naughty things? How often does it happen? What are I and other family members doing when the misbehavior begins? What does the dog do just prior to her misbehaving? And, finally, think about how you respond to the dog when she commits those unwanted habits.

I have five steps to successfully change bad habits into good ones. Applied carefully, they can turn a dog with a disagreeable wetting habit into a happy, self-confident dog that never wets submissively.

1. Anticipate when the unwanted behavior is about to happen. Answering the aforementioned questions will clue you into the triggers that signal your dog to have an accident.

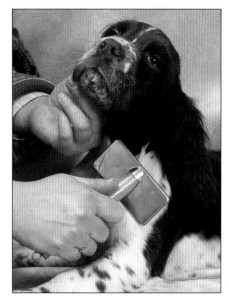

You can distract the pup away from bad behavior with grooming. Many dogs like the one-on-one bonding of grooming time.

2. Distract your dog by getting her involved in some activity she enjoys. Taking a walk, getting brushed, playing with a toy and having some cuddle time with a family member are all activities that will take the dog's mind off the unwanted behavior and provide her with the positive attention she needs. The secret to successful distraction is that you must employ the distraction *before* she begins the unwanted behavior. If you try to distract her once she has begun to show submissive behavior, then you'll only be rewarding her for exhibiting the rolling over and wetting habit.

3. Ignore undesirable behaviors. Provide substitutions

gets attention when she's quiet in her crate.

When your meal is finished, release her from the crate and praise lavishly to let her know she's been very good. In addition, you can call her to the kitchen for a special treat to help emphasize how pleased you are that she was good and quiet while you were eating dinner. Put a treat in her bowl.

4. Respond promptly to any signs of unwanted behavior. Don't wait until she's in the middle of doing something naughty to stop her. The moment she looks like she's about to steal your shoe, respond to the intent of the act by changing her focus. Give her one of her own toys to play with rather than yell at her to leave your shoes alone. Remember, you can only alter the submissive wetting by *not* yelling at her.

5. Praise her when she acts positively in a certain situation. Be quick to tell her how pleased you are with her behavior. For example, let's say she begins to grab your pant leg to play tug-of-war. Distract her with a question: "Where's your fluffy toy?" or "Do you want to go out?"

The moment she responds to your question by turning away from your leg, let her know what a good girl she is.

The crate must be the pup's "happy place," never used for punishment but instead used to shape good behavior.

to replace those unwanted acts. For example, if you know that she demands attention when you're eating your dinner, change things around and give her some time out with a biscuit and a special toy in her crate while you enjoy your dinner in peace.

Place the crate in a room other than where you are eating. Not only can she hear you, she can smell you and your T-bone. If she fusses to get out and join you at the table, pretend you don't even hear a barking dog. Remember, ignore the fussing. Put a towel over the crate to make it dark so she'll fall asleep instead of sitting there, begging for your dinner and your attention. A few nights of ignoring her noise and she'll figure out that she only

Turning away from her tug-of-war target and focusing on you will earn her positive attention because you won't become angry with her. If you don't act negatively toward her, she won't roll over and wet the floor. That's what you call a win/win situation.

Changing an annoying submissive behavior into a positive reaction to you will take some time. It won't happen in two days, so don't expect a miracle. However, being consistent and praising the positive aspects of your interactions with your dog will slowly but surely reduce the number of times she wets the floor and acts fearful.

Psychologists and behavior consultants believe that most unwanted behaviors of dogs are caused by humans. In the majority of cases, owners either don't know how to handle undesirable dog behaviors or they respond emotionally rather than rationally to their pet's naughty or unwanted habits.

Taking the time to develop a series of corrective steps to use in retraining your dog will ultimately pay big dividends for you both. Once you've thought out how you'll handle a given situation, employ the program consistently and allow a positive attitude to set the tone of modifying the dog's behavior. Believing that you can achieve your goals for your dog will have a large influence on a successful outcome.

Don't be shy about really celebrating your dog's successes...go ahead, have a happy house-training party!

INDEX